TREATISE ON LAWS
by
Matthew J. Ogden

© July 23, 2023
Matthew J. Ogden
Pottstown, Pennsylvania

ISBN: 9781312302297

TABLE OF CONTENTS

Chapter I. General Precepts — *Page 3*

Chapter II. The Natural Law — *Page 31*

Chapter III. The Old Law — *Page 142*

Chapter IV. The New Law — *Page 202*

Chapter V. Human Law — *Page 331*

CHAPTER I.
GENERAL PRECEPTS

In order to properly understand law, it is necessary to consider the definition of law. A law is defined as a general rule or precept established by a legitimate authority for the sake of upholding the good. As it is evident, there are several different parts to this definition, each of which can be considered on its own in order to better understand the nature of law in general. The first and most essential element of a law is that it is a rule or precept. These two terms mean the same thing. A rule is a kind of measure that establishes the way that something is or ought to be. At the same time, a rule is more than a measure, since it also carries with it an imperative quality. Hence when it is said that a law is a kind of rule or precept, this means that it imposes a kind of order on the thing itself. This is the most necessary quality of the law itself. This is the matter of the law, which is what the law is in itself.

  The next part of a law is that it is established in some way. Now this means that the rule or precept that is the law itself inheres in some way to the thing that the law itself governs. Hence when it is said that animals in the created world operate according to laws that depend upon their nature, this means that the law to which they adhere is a part of them in some way, so that it prescribes the things that they do. So the way that they interact with other living things, or even the ways that the animal body itself operates to keep the animal alive, are both ways that it can be said that the law has been established in some manner. The prescriptive nature of law also means that there is at least a logical possibility that the thing that the law governs can be other than what it is. This is what makes the law itself to be necessary in the first place. If a thing cannot be other than what it is, there is no need for the law itself. With the possible exception of the laws of logic, there is no way that a law can prescribe something that can only be in one way. This means that what the law itself has prescribed is necessarily possible at the same time. The law concerns only possibilities. If something is wholly impossible, there is no way that the law can address it at all. Hence when a law is established, it only concerns what can be done. At the same time, the law separates what ought to be done from what ought not to be done.

For a law to be established means that there has to be a legitimate power to establish the law in the first place. Now since a law is necessarily a rule or precept that establishes limits for a certain object, the one who makes the law must necessarily have a mind that is capable of knowing the situation for the thing itself that the law controls. This means that only an intelligent being can possibly make a law. Thus when it is considered that there is a natural law, it is the case that there has to be a mind that created the natural law to be what it is. The natural law presupposes the intelligent mind to make the law in the first place. The intelligent mind Who made the natural law is God. It is evident that God has a mind that is capable of knowing things because there are other intelligent beings that exist, and what is intelligent is higher than what is not also intelligent. Now God is above all of His creation because He alone is the first cause of all other things that exist, and the cause of a thing being such is yet more so. As there are other intelligent beings that exist, the intelligent beings are higher than what is not intelligent, and God is above all of His creation, it can thus be said that God has a mind capable of knowing things. And it is also the case that God knows all things that can possibly be known through His own essence. The Divine essence is the first cause of all other things that exist, and the effect must be in the cause in order for it to be the effect of that cause. Hence the essences of all created natures exist in God in a more perfect manner than they exist even in themselves. So when God turns to understand His own essence, He sees the perfection of all other things that exist within His essence. God knows the reality of all other things that exist by subtracting from the perfection of those things as they exist in His essence. This is how God knows all things through His essence. So if God is intelligent and knows all things through His own essence, it can thus be said that God has the ability to make laws for His creation. This is how God is the origin of all laws. As the effect must be in the cause in order for it to be the effect of that cause, the nature of law as something that exists in the created world cannot be fully understood without reference to God as the first cause of all other things that exist.

God's relevance to law is even more apparent considering the end for which the law itself exists. The final part of the definition of law is that it takes place for the sake of some good. Hence to properly understand the end of law, and thus the nature of the law itself, one must know the nature of the good. Things are defined by their ends, and the end of law is the good to which the law itself is directed. Now being is the same thing as goodness because the good is desirable, and all things desire being above all else, since it is from being that they come into other good things. So being is the same thing as goodness.

And the Divine essence is existence Itself. The things that are caused come by means of their own causation into an existence that already exists itself. But God has no cause, as He alone is the first cause. So there is no existence that is prior to God's essence. This means that essence and existence are the same in God alone, meaning that the Divine essence is existence Itself. And since being is the same thing as goodness and the Divine essence is existence Itself, God alone is essentially good. This means that since God alone is essentially good, all other good things that exist are directed in some way to God as their ultimate end. This includes the different kinds of laws that exist in the created world.

It is important to consider that God alone is essentially good while all of the other things that exist in the created world are good only by their participation in God. Thus if being is the same thing as goodness, the other things that exist in the created world are sustained in being as what they are by the Divine essence Itself. This is how it is said that all that God made in the created world is good. Since what is essentially so is more so than what is only by participation, it can be said that God is greater than all other things that exist. This is how God is the ultimate end for all things that exist. The end for things can be either proximate or ultimate. The proximate end means that a thing is the end for some other thing, but still stands in relation to something beyond it as a means to that thing. The ultimate end means that there is nothing beyond it. Now since things work for the sake of the good because the good is desirable, God alone is the ultimate end for all things because there is nothing greater than God. Yet the created subject can still seek created goods as a proximate end on the way to come closer to God as the ultimate end.

Insofar as law is concerned, the law is one of the ways that the object can be moved closer to God as the only essential good and as the ultimate end for all things that exist. And God is the ultimate end for all other things that exist. It was said that God alone is essentially good because being is the same thing as goodness and the Divine essence is existence Itself. This means that all that God does is always good, as the effect must be in the cause in order for it to be the effect of that cause, and there is nothing in God that is not the essential goodness of the Divine essence. So all that God does is always good. This means that the end of all that God does must be the greatest possible good in every case, as things are defined by their ends, and all that God does is always good. Since the Divine essence Itself is essentially good, this means that God does all that He does in every case for the sake of His own essence. This is how God is both the beginning and the end of all other things that exist. So when it is said that the end of law is a possible good, this means that the law is directed in some way to God as the ultimate end of all things and the only essential good that exists.

Now since God is the ultimate end of all other things that exist, this means that all of God's creation will eventually be reconciled back to God in the end, each thing in its own way. This is consistent with how God created the entire world in the first place in order to share His own essential goodness with all things each according to their nature as what they are. God shares His own essential goodness with all things when He sustains them all in being as what they are by His very essence, and He also does this when He works to perfect all things that exist by bringing them back to His essence in the end. The different created natures that exist all share in the essential goodness of God in these different ways. And the way that God brings all things back to Himself as the ultimate end for the created world concerns law, since law exists for the sake of a good which is the proper end of the law itself.

There are certain ways in which a law has to be intelligible to the one who observes the law itself. This depends upon the nature of the law and the object bound by the law. Hence it can be said that non-rational animals are bound by certain laws that govern their behavior, but at the same time they do not have the ability to understand the law itself that moves them. The non-rational intellect cannot understand universal things, meaning that the non-rational animal has no ability to fully comprehend the abstract laws that move it. The non-rational animal might have some limited comprehension of the laws that it obeys, but it cannot understand the law itself. It can only understand the particular ways in which the law affects it. Thus it can be taken as a law that the animal body does what it can to sustain the individual animal. So the animal will seek out food, water, shelter, and other things in order to continue to live. But while the animal works in these ways for the sake of its own survival, it does not fully understand the need to do these things in order to continue to live. The animals knows that it needs them, but that the animal thus operates according to a law in this way is beyond the limits of its intelligence.

      The case is different for men because men possess a rational intellect and free will. The rational intellect of men can understand universal things, which means that men can figure out the overall law that governs the ways that things operate in the created world. So men have the ability to know the laws that rule them and other created natures. They also have a free will that derives from the rational intellect. The will that derives from the rational intellect is necessarily a free will. The rational intellect can make complex distinctions, which means that the men can choose among the different things that were distinguished using the will that derives from it. As the will has more choices, it is necessarily a free will, where choice is the essence of freedom. So if men have a rational intellect and free will, they can understand laws. This means that if men are to use their free will to obey laws, they must first understand them. So if an authority imposes on a man a law by which the man is bound through his free will, the man must know the nature of the law itself. If the man does not know that he is bound in his free will to a particular law, he cannot make an effort to act accordingly. This means that if he violates the law that the authority had imposed on him, he cannot be held to account for it. The man bound by the law itself did not know that he had to follow the law, meaning that if he violated the law, this did not directly come from his free will. The man did not intend to transgress the law that the authority had imposed on him. From this it is evident that a law has to be known in order for the rational subject to be bound by it in his free will. For this reason as well, it is also proper that the law that binds the rational subject is clear and easy for him to understand. If the law is difficult for him to understand, he will have greater difficulty obeying it. This also means that any transgression of the law that takes place is not with the same culpability as if the law itself was clear and the man was able to fully understand the way that the law was binding upon him in the first place.

It is the nature of laws that they can only bind events that are to take place in the future. Law is concerned with contingency, meaning that laws are about what can or cannot happen. Yet this exclusively refers to the future because the past cannot be changed. Now it is possible for men to pass laws that concern the interpretation of past events, but this still refers to what will take place going forth into the future. It may change the ways that the past events are understood, but the understanding itself that is changed is necessarily in the future. Hence it is impossible for any laws that exist to concern the past in this manner. This is even the case for God, because God cannot change the past. God sustains the entire created world in being as what it is. Now since God is eternal, He sees all of time at once. And for God to change the past in some way would mean that the past was what it was and yet also was not what it was. This is a contradiction, meaning that not even God has the ability to change the past from what actually occurred.

Beyond the intelligibility of law and the possibility of observing what the law has ordered, it is the case that a law imposes an obligation on what is bound by the law. This relates to how law exists for the sake of some good. If the thing bound by the law does not act in accord with the law itself, then it does not come into the good that was possible to it in the given case. So when the subject whose acts are ordered by the law itself fails to observe the law, this means that it suffers from the lack of the possible good. This can come about in two different ways. First, this can happen inherently because of the consequence of the law itself that was not followed. Hence if an animal needs food and water, but fails to seek out these things for some reason, it may die without them. The loss of life is the inevitable consequence of the animal not seeking the things that it needed to maintain life. Second, this can happen because the subject who failed to obey the law was punished for not obeying it. It was said that a law has to be promulgated by some authority in order for it to be a legitimate law. And the authority who is the source of the law can impose certain penalties on those bound by the law in order to compel observance. This means that some possible good for the one who defies the law will be intentionally taken away as the consequence for the law itself being ignored. And since the authority exists for the sake of upholding the good through the law, the nature of the good that is the proper end of the particular law may be so important that to ignore or contradict the law requires some kind of punishment.

      This concerns the four different functions of law itself. Thus far the definition of law itself has been considered, as well as the things that are essential to the law such as contingency. But it is also necessary to see what the law actually does when the different conditions to make the law itself are observed. The four different functions of law are to command, to permit, to prohibit, and to punish. It is evident that of these four different conditions, two of them are more moderate and the other two are more severe. Hence there is a degree that exists in the functions of law. When the authority commands observance of a law, this means that the subject must do what the law ordered. Not to do what the law had ordered means that the subject necessarily failed to work in accord with the good that is the end of the law itself. For a law to command, the good that is the end of the law itself must be of great importance, so that if the law was not there to command the particular act, there would be great suffering among those who are bound by the law itself. As the law must work for the sake of the greatest possible good in the given case, it makes sense that matters of great importance require the subject bound by the law to be commanded.

But there are other matters of lesser importance among the subjects who are bound by laws, meaning that in such cases the authority who makes the laws can permit the subjects to do certain things. In the case of men in particular, God gave men their free will in order for them to work more efficiently for the sake of the greatest possible good on their own. When the men use their free will to work for the sake of the greatest possible good, they become the proximate cause of the good that they do. God Himself is the ultimate cause thereof because God gave the men their free will in the first place. So when the men use their free will for the sake of a good, they can become better than they were before, meaning that they can have more delight overall from being the proximate cause of the good that they did. Since men can use their free will for the sake of their own good, it is proper that men are permitted to work for the sake of the good in some ways without being commanded.

Yet it is also the nature of human free will that men cannot lose their free will insofar as it is one of the qualities that makes them to be men. Men can lose the ability to use their free will through disease or injury, so that they no longer have the free ability to do as they please. And other men might try to compel the free will of different men so that the different men do as they please. But when other men try to force the free will of men, the free will of the men being forced necessarily escapes from the power of the man applying the force to the other man. For example, if one man tries to compel another man to do something with his hands, the other man whose hands are moved are not moved by the man himself, but by the man who tries to compel him. Hence the act done does not come from the man being compelled, but rather from the man who compels. So while the man who compels wants the other man to do these things with his hands, it is the man who compels that actually does the act. In this sense no man can take hold of another man's free will and compel him to do what he wants. Men can use incitements to try to get other men to do what they please, either by offering them good things or threatening them with bad things. Yet if the man either bribed or threatened goes along with what the other man compels him to do, he still uses his own free will. He has decided in his rational intellect to comply with the man that compels him. And it can also be said that the man who compels reduces the culpability of the man compelled by the way that he tries to move the man to do as he wills. So if a man is moved by bribery or threats to act in a certain way, what the man did by his free will under the imposed bribery or threats was less freely done. Hence any praise or blame that might come to the man compelled for what he did will necessarily be less than it would be if he did it otherwise.

Similarly if a man does not know certain things that he ought to know in order for him to act in a certain way, this means that he lacked the proper intention when he did the act itself. Not knowing what he did when he did it means that he cannot be held formally responsible for the act itself. The man did the matter of the act in particular, but he did not know when he did it what was the end for which the act had been intended. This means that he could not formally intend the act itself when he did it. Hence it would not make sense to hold him fully accountable for what he did. It is clear from this that ignorance excuses from culpability. But ignorance itself can be considered either invincible or vincible. If a man does not know what he can know because it was impossible for him to know it, the man is invincibly ignorant, meaning that what the man does through the invincible ignorance is not subject to either praise or blame. Yet if a man avoids knowing something that he could know so that he is not responsible for what he does, he can still be held to account all the same. The man cannot be held to account for the thing done, but he can be held to account for the way that he avoided knowing what he needed to know to do the good in the given case.

So when the authority makes the laws, permission is one of the ways that the authority can work for the good of those subject to the law. For an authority to order all good things by command would take away some of the free will of the subjects, meaning that they would not have the same delight from doing the good. The good would come from them less because they were commanded to do it, meaning that insofar as the law itself was concerned, the choice was not their own. Since the law exists to work for the sake of the good, and men can often work better for their own good when this is freely done, it makes sense that the authority responsible for making the laws would not command all good acts. This way the men subject to the law can work more for the sake of the good on their own without being compelled by the command of the authority. Hence it is proper that command should only be used in the law in the most serious of cases, so that the men can still exercise their free will as God intended. For an authority to command all good things to be done by the men would mean that the authority had not only contradicted the nature of man as a being endowed with free will, but he would also thus contradict God's will in giving men their free will in the first place. For which reason the exercise of a man's free will within proper limits is an essential part of all laws that govern men. No authority can or ought to command all good things to be done, even if the particular ends sought through the laws themselves are actually for the sake of an objective good.

The laws must recognize the nature of the subjects bound by the law, meaning that any laws that bind men must take into account their free will. But while men have free will so that they can freely work for the sake of the greatest possible good in the given case, it is also possible at the same time that men can misuse their free will to do evil. It was said that it is the nature of free will that the subject can do other than what he does. Hence while men have their free will to work for the good, that they can also use their free will for evil is part of what makes them free. A will that can only act for the sake of one thing is not a free will at all. Thus while God gave men their free will to work for the sake of the greatest possible good, men still have the ability to also act for the sake of evil as well. This does not mean that to act for the sake of an evil is ever permissible. It only means that this is still possible to men by their own free will.

Now since the law exists for the sake of the good, and the law also deals with contingencies, it is necessary that laws prohibit some things in addition to being able to command or permit. This is one of the four functions of law. And the law above all else prohibits evil as part of the way that the law works for the sake of some good. Since being is the same thing as goodness, evil is contrary to the good, meaning that the lack of the being that can be present but is not present in the given case. So when something works for the sake of some good in the given case, the result is that more being results from what was possible in the given case. This does not have to mean that the being that results is quantitatively more than was actually present before the event, because it is also possible that the being to result can simply be the preservation of some being that was already there. These are two ways that more being can result, meaning that the event was for the sake of the good. But when evil occurs, the being that results is less than what was possible in the given case. This can mean that some being that was actually there is taken away, or it can mean a greater quantity of being was possible but still did not result in the end. Since law is for the sake of the good, it makes sense that law would also work to uphold the good by prohibiting what may take away from the good. This is how this is one of the functions of law.

That the law can prohibit the evil from happening does not have to mean that the evil will still not result. Concerning the free will of men, men might not see the prohibition of the law itself as a reason not to do what the law forbids. In which cases it is necessary for the law to also punish men who do not obey the precepts of the law. To punish someone means that the subject loses some good for the sake of what he did. Since the effect must be in the cause in order for it to be the effect of that cause, it can thus be said that the man who fails to do the good in accord with the law must also lack some of the good within him if the lack of the good came from him. The lack of the good to come from him was the effect and the man himself was the cause thereof. So when the man did what lacked some of the good because he lacks some good in himself, it makes sense that he loses some good for the good that he does not have in himself. The man does not deserve the good that would otherwise have come to him because of the way that he lacks some of the good in himself. And since the authority who makes the laws is charged with upholding the good for all of the subjects who are bound by the law itself, the authority can impose certain punishments on the man who violated the law by what he did. Thus the authority gave the man who violated the law what he deserved, and at the same time the authority might dissuade other men from also violating the law in the same way. The punishment for the violation of a law can deter other men from also violating the law, though this is not the primary purpose of the punishment itself. Even if no one is deterred from violating a law by the imposed punishment, it is still necessary to punish the man who violated the law in the interest of justice.

Justice is essential to the operation of the law. Justice means that an object gets what it deserves as what it is. In this sense justice is based on equality, so that the thing gets the equal of what it deserves according to its nature. Now justice can be divided into three different kinds. First, there is commutative justice, which means that two or more things get what is equal to each other. Second, there is distributive justice, which means that a thing gets the equal of what it deserves for what it is. Third, there is retributive justice, which means that a thing loses some good for it because it did not deserve to get the good in the given case. Punishment is retributive justice, because the punishment takes away a possible good from the subject for the way that the subject does not deserve to receive some good in the given case.

It might seem that since the law as such works for the sake of the greatest possible good in each case that it is contrary to the law to impose punishments. Punishments take away some good from the subject, meaning that the punishments appear to contradict the way that the law is for the greater good. But this cannot be said. Punishment works for the sake of a greater good insofar as it is in accord with justice. Hence while the matter of the punishment is the deprivation of a possible good, the form of the punishment is that the object gets what it deserves. This is what is good for the object itself, which is the way that punishment upholds the greater good. In terms of human society, it can be said that the greater good is the good for many men as opposed to one man. Hence it may be in accord with the greater good for one man to lose some good for what he did so that justice is upheld for the rest of the men in the society who did suffer or would suffer if the man who was punished was allowed to get away with what he did with impunity. This is one of the ways that a punishment can work for the sake of the greater good overall despite how the matter thereof is the loss of a possible good.

Hence equality is the proper end of justice, and the equality for which justice works can take these three different forms. When justice works for the sake of some equality, and the equality is for the sake of a greater good, it can be said that the equality itself in this case is called a right. A right is the establishment of some kind of equality for the sake of upholding the common good. Since the end of the right is the common good to which it is directed, it can be said that rights by their nature as circumstantial, insofar as the common good can be served in different ways for men in different societies based on the particular circumstances. Hence what may be a right in one case may not also be a right in another case, perhaps even within the same society. Men are not all the same, and the societies that they form are also not all the same, meaning that the understanding of a particular right in one time and place may not be strictly applicable in another.

But while the concept of a right in general is inherently circumstantial, there are some cases in which the circumstances concerning the right itself are always the same. These rights concern human nature. Human nature is the same for all men as men. If this was not the case, it would be impossible to refer to them all as men. While men may differ in particular ways, such as according to abilities or their race, this does not mean that they are not all men. Insofar as they are all men, what pertains to them as men is the same for all of them. Thus there are some circumstances when the way to uphold the greatest possible good for them is always the same regardless of time and place. This does not mean that the right itself inheres in human nature, since there is nothing in human nature as such to assume that certain equalities are necessarily part of the men themselves. This would make it possible for different men to claim that anything that they happen to desire would necessarily be a right only because they thought it was good for them, which would be absurd. So while men always benefit in the same ways in some cases because their human nature is the same for all men, this does not detract from the way that rights as such are circumstantial. The circumstances are merely the same because of the particular case. Yet if the case can differ in other ways, then the particular right that pertains to the case itself would not be the same for all men across all times and places.

Thus rights and justice are necessary for the law to work for the sake of the greater good. The equality that is the end of justice must work for the sake of the good in order for the law to fulfill its proper function. The equality that works for the sake of the good in this way is called a right. But there are some cases when the proper order of justice does not work for the sake of the greatest possible good in the given case. In those cases it is necessary to dispense with the order of justice and instead to use mercy to bring about the greatest possible good that is the regular end of justice. Thus it can be said that justice is not so much the end of law as a means to the end, where the end of the law is the good itself that justice upholds. Now mercy is to spare a thing from the evil that it deserves as what it is. It would seem that mercy and justice are opposed to each other, since the object either gets or does not get what it deserves in the given case. In some sense this can be said. But it can instead be said that mercy adds to justice where justice fails to work as it ordinarily does for the sake of the greatest possible good. Men can and ought to take into account the times that justice does not work for the sake of the greatest possible good when they administer justice for the sake of the common good.

      Hence mercy can be considered a dispensation from justice. Dispensations are part of the way that the law works for the sake of the greatest possible good. This is called equity. It is not possible for human law to fully take account all future contingencies that may occur within human society, because their total number would be infinite. And it is also the case that the different circumstances in each case might mitigate the culpability of the man who did the act itself that the law regulates. This was already shown concerning vincible and invincible ignorance. Now since the possible circumstances in determining how to apply the law to different cases are potentially infinite, there are cases when it is better to dispense with the ordinary rule of the law itself in order to uphold the greater good. This means that the law in the particular case does not work in the way that was intended for the sake of the greater good. The law may ordinarily work for the good, but it happens that it does not work for the good in this particular case, and that the men who made the law could not have possibly foreseen this particular circumstance arising under the law when the law itself was promulgated. This is why equity is a necessary part of the law. But given that the law is there to uphold the greater good, and the particular law mostly does work for the sake of the greater good, the men responsible for the application of the laws should be careful when they choose to dispense with the law for the sake of a greater good. The good that the equity upholds should be readily apparent in the given case so that this practice does not lend itself to corruption in the application of the law.

The making of human laws must always take into account the role of proper virtue. Virtue is defined as to act for the sake of the greatest possible good in the given case. And it was said that God alone is essentially good because being is the same thing as goodness and the Divine essence is existence Itself, meaning that God ought to be the ultimate end of all virtue. But virtue can also be taken in terms of its proximate ends with God Himself as the ultimate end. Now since law is for the sake of the greatest possible good, and virtue also works for the greatest possible good, it is necessarily the case that the laws that men make to govern human societies are based on virtue. The reason that some acts in human society are necessarily prohibited as crimes is because they are immoral. Killing, rape, or theft are all prohibited by societies because they are immoral acts. It is possible to debate the limits of what may constitute these different acts in particular cases, but it cannot be denied that they are illegal insofar as they are immoral. Yet at the same time, this does not mean that all immoral acts necessarily have to be illegal. As it was said, the law properly takes into account human free will, and human free will necessarily includes the ability to do evil. Hence it makes sense that human societies allow men some latitude in acts even when it is possible that the acts themselves are evil.

At the same time, not all of the acts that human society considers against the law have to be immoral. There are times when human society will enforce certain customs that are not inherently based in morality, but which pertain in some way to the public order. Since it benefits men to live in an ordered society, the authority responsible for making the laws can prohibit certain acts that are contrary to order in some manner. So while law generally is based in morality, there are some immoral acts that are not illegal, and there are some illegal acts that are not necessarily immoral. The former can be determined based on prudence, while the observance of the latter can carry with it a moral obligation of sorts, since the men in the human society should work for the common good, and the order upheld by the law is in the interest of the common good even if the way that the law upholds the order is either arbitrary or based solely on custom. Thus it is evident that some things are immoral in themselves while other things can be taken as immoral only insofar as they are prohibited by the law for the sake of public order. But in the latter case, the law is determined only by custom rather than by some other moral imperative.

These are the different general concepts that need to be understood before considering the different kinds of law that exist and the objects governed by the laws themselves. It is clear from what has been said that all law has its origin in God both as the first cause for all other things that exist and as the ultimate end to Whom all things are directed by their very nature. Now since God alone is essentially good, and the greater good is the end of law, law concerns God no less than any of the other things that exist in the created world. This is inherent in the definition of law. It has also been considered the different ways that the law functions for the sake of the greater good, as well as the various related concepts that allow the law to fulfill this purpose, such as equality, rights, justice, and mercy. Since these general concepts have been considered, it is possible to individually address the different kinds of law that exist in the created world. These are the natural law, the Divine law, and the human law. All three of these emanate from the eternal law that exists in the Divine essence Itself, and all three of them must confirm to the eternal law in order for them to be considered legitimate laws. These are the topics that will now be considered.

CHAPTER II.
THE NATURAL LAW

Having considered the general precepts of law, the things that are common to all different kinds of law as such, it is proper to move onto the different kinds of law in particular. Now the four different kinds of law are the eternal law, the natural law, the Divine law, and human law. And all four of these derive their being from God, but in different ways. This is because God alone is the first cause of all other things that exist. The effect must be in the cause in order for it to be the effect of that cause. As God alone is the first cause of all other things that exist, this means that the essences of all different created natures exist in God preeminently and in a more perfect manner than they exist even within themselves. They exist in God more than they exist in themselves because the cause of a thing being such is yet more so. Hence in order for all things to derive their being from God as the first cause thereof, they are necessarily contained in their perfection within the Divine essence Itself.

This includes the four different kinds of law that were said to exist. The eternal law above all exists in the Divine essence, and is the basis for the other three kinds of law. This has to do with the nature of law in general. Law was said to be a rule that is established by an authority for the sake of upholding some good. Now God alone is essentially good because being is the same thing as goodness and the Divine essence is existence Itself. This means that all that comes from God is also good, since the effect must be in the cause in order for it to be the effect of that cause, and there is nothing in God that is not the essential goodness of the Divine essence. So all of the other things that exist are good because God made them, sustains them in being, and they exist in their perfection within the Divine essence Itself. Now since the perfection of all other things that exist is present in the Divine essence, the rules that make them what they are also are present there as well. This is how the eternal law is a sovereign type that exists in God.

And it is the case that the eternal law as such cannot suffer from any kind of change. This can be said for three reasons. First, the eternal law exists in the Divine essence Itself, and God alone is eternal. Eternity is the state where a thing exists as simultaneously whole. Time is the distinction of before and after in things that are moved. But God alone is unmoved because He alone is the first mover. It takes a prior mover to move something, and there is nothing prior to

God because He alone is the first mover. This means that God alone is unmoved in His essence. Since God alone is unmoved, God does not exist in time. Hence the Divine essence is perfectly whole. The essences of different created natures are all moved in some way or to some degree. This is because there is something prior to them in order to move them, either God as the ultimate mover or some other created goods as the proximate movers thereof. So the being of the different created natures is always discursive in some way. As God alone is unmoved, the Divine essence alone exists as simultaneously whole. And since the eternal law is the sovereign type that exists in God, this means that the eternal law cannot change. Change is a kind of motion, and God alone is unmoved, meaning that the eternal law in God is also unmoved as well.

Second, the eternal law is unchanged because it exists in God, and God alone is absolutely perfect. Perfection is the state where a thing lacks nothing. Perfection can be considered as being either absolute or relative. Absolute perfection means that a thing lacks nothing at all to its being. Relative perfection means that a thing lacks nothing that is possible to it according to its nature as what it is. Now God alone is absolutely perfect because His essence is the first cause of all other things that exist, and the effect must reside in the cause in order for it to be the effect of that cause. So the essences of all created natures thus exist in God, which is how God is absolutely perfect. God is all good things in His own essence. Created natures can be relatively perfect, but God alone as the first cause of all other things is absolutely perfect. Since the eternal law exists in the Divine essence Itself as the sovereign type of all law, and the Divine essence is absolutely perfect, this means that there is no way that the eternal law can ever be changed. It cannot become more perfect, since it exists in God Who alone is absolutely perfect. And it cannot become less perfect because all that God does is always perfect because His essence is perfect, and the effect resembles the cause in order for it to be the effect of that cause. So if God alone is absolutely perfect, then there is no way that anything imperfect can ever possibly come from God. Even the imperfections that God allows to exist in the fallen world are for the sake of some greater good that would not have been possible but for the way that some lesser good was already lacking in the given case. This is how all that God does is perfect. So the eternal law in God cannot be made more perfect and cannot fall into any imperfection either. This is one of the ways that the eternal law is unchanged.

Third, it can be said that the Divine will for all things is immutable, meaning that the eternal law according to which God governs all things cannot change either. It takes a greater power to overcome a lesser one, and there is no power greater than God, meaning that what God wills for all things is always fulfilled. And since God knows all things through His own essence, which was already explained, God cannot change His mind about what He does, so that what He already did was not as good as it could have been. This means that the eternal law by which God governs the entire created world cannot change to be something other than what it is. These are the ways that it can be said that the eternal law is not subject to change.

At the same time, this does not mean that things in the created world that God governs are also not subject to change. It is evident from the external senses that God does allow there to be changes that take place in the created world. These changes are governed by the eternal law, which itself does not change. God does all that He does for the sake of the greatest possible good, which means that whatever happens in the created world is directed to some good in the end, and thus also to the Divine essence Itself as the ultimate end for all things, since God alone is the highest good because He alone is essentially good. And when God allows evil to exist, it is so that He can bring some good even out of evil. But the eternal law itself, as the plan from which all of these changes take place, is itself unchanged. This is made more apparent from how God exists outside of time because He alone is eternal. This means that God sees all of time at once. So God can see the past, present, and future so that they all appear to Him as simultaneous events. Hence God can make it so that one thing happens in one place at one time, but then something different happens in the same place at a different time or at the same time but in a different place. This is how there is no contradiction in what happens, and also no contradiction in the unchanging nature of the eternal law governing a fallen world that experiences changes.

That the eternal law can be called a sovereign type existing in God does not change that the Divine essence is perfectly simple. For the Divine essence to be simple means that It is not composed of parts. The parts of a thing are determined by what caused them. But God has no cause, as He is the first cause of all other things that exist. So God cannot have parts either, which is how the Divine essence is perfectly simple. So when it is said that there are different essences that exist within the Divine essence, this does not mean that God is composed of parts. All of the different essences of created natures that exist in the Divine essence do so as the essence Itself. Hence when it is said that God has attributes, the attributes are the same as the essence Itself. And this can also be said for the eternal law as the sovereign type that exists in God. Insofar as the eternal law exists in God, the eternal law is the same as the Divine essence, which can also be said for all of the other attributes that are given to the Divine essence.

Thus the eternal law is the basis for the other three kinds of law that exist, which are the natural law, the Divine law, and human law. Having addressed the eternal law, it is necessary to consider these other three kinds of law, beginning with the natural law. The natural law is the law that inheres in the nature of different created things. Hence it is evident considering the way that different creatures exist how they ought to operate. And just as the nature of the creature in general makes evident what the creature itself ought to do, the same can be said for the different parts of the creature itself. Thus when considering the nature of men, it is evident from the different parts of the human nature how these parts ought to operate and to which objects they may properly be directed. All that takes place in the created world acts for the sake of a good. Hence the end for which motion exists necessarily has an element of the good about it. The converse can also be said, so that the good has the nature of an end. In the case of men, it is possible to see from the various faculties of men the good to which these faculties are directed. And if the different parts of the man are used for some purpose that is separated from the end for which the faculty exists, then the act itself that takes place through the faculty is lacking in due rectitude.

Now it was said that law is a rule that exists for the sake of some good, so that the good is the end for the rule itself. And it was said that virtue is, by definition, to act for the sake of the greatest possible good in every case. Since law and virtue have the same end, this is how there is a necessary connection between them. Thus what is done in accord with virtue is also in accord with some kind of law at the same time. As the law is for the sake of the good as the end thereof, when the good as the end of the law is not sought through this or that particular kind of act, the act itself is necessarily a sin. Sin is to choose a lesser good over the greatest possible good in the given case. The lesser good, as lesser, lacks some being that can be there, and being was said to be the same thing as goodness. This is what is meant when the act is lacking in due rectitude. There is some being that is necessary to the act itself for the act to be complete, but this being is lacking to the act. And the lack of the being in the act makes the act to be a sin. Thus if men as the subject of different kinds of law are able to receive the fullest amount of the good in the end for what they do in the given case, they must act in accord with virtue. When men act in accord with virtue, this means that they adhere to one of the three different kinds of law, and thus always to the eternal law as the sovereign type in God and as the origin of all of the other kinds of law.

The natural law in particular binds not only men, but also all of the other things that exist in the created world. Thus it can be said that all created natures, insofar as they are moved for the sake of an end, are moved by and through the natural law when they work for the greatest good possible to them as what they are. And the end that is the greatest possible good for them can be determined from the nature of the thing itself and the ways that it is moved for the sake of an end. But at the same time, it is also the case that not all that is moved in the fallen world necessarily works in every case for the greatest good that is the proper end of the movement. It is possible for men to observe the ways that different things in the natural world ought to work for the sake of a particular good as the end thereof, but those things still fail to do so in this or that case. This is one of the consequences of the Fall. When the first men committed the original sin from the temptation of the devil, they not only corrupted human nature, but also the rest of the created world. Thus it is possible to observe the ways that things in nature do not always work for the sake of the good that is evidently the end to which this or that object may be moved. Yet it was said that God allows evil to exist in order to bring some good even out of evil, where the good that results in the end would not have been possible but for the way that the evil was present in the first place. As God does all that He does in every case for the sake of the greatest possible good, men can be content to know that God will use the evils from which they suffer for a greater good. And if they remain in proper virtue, and continue to observe the different kinds of law to the fullest extent of their ability, they can benefit in some way from the ways that they suffered from the lack of a possible good. Hence they can even come closer to God by the ways that they remained committed to doing the good despite the difficulty that arose from the evil that they had to suffer.

That the created world can suffer from transgressions from the natural law at times does not undermine the ways that men can still see from the nature of different objects how the object itself ought to work for the sake of some particular good as what it is. That it does not do this in every case does not negate the general rule that this or that way is the way for the object to come into the good. It also does not compromise the ability of men to find out what is the end for which the object should act in different cases for the sake of its own good. Hence while it is possible that an animal body might have difficulty digesting food, this does not mean that the digestive system of the animal is not there to break down the foods consumed into their constituent parts in order to keep the animal body alive. The failure of the created nature to obtain to the good as the proper end in every case does not mean that the end is not the end after all, or that the parts of the created nature involved in the movement exist for the sake of some other purpose.

Hence the natural law necessarily governs the entire created world. And while all of the different things in the created world are directed to some good as the proper end thereof, it can also be said that the natural law itself is directed to an end. The proximate end of the natural law is to uphold the existing created good for the different objects that God has made. And the ultimate end for the natural law is God Himself, since it was said that God is both the beginning and the end of all other things that exist. So the good that takes place in the created world in accord with the natural law can lead back to God as the ultimate end thereof. But this is necessarily indirect, as most of the different created natures that exist are moved for the sake of some created good at the same time. This is clear even from human observation of things that exist within the created world.

Now since men are part of the created world, it is evident that men are also governed by the natural law at the same time. This is no less the case than it is for anything else that exists. And since the natural law, like all of the other kinds of law, exists for the sake of some greater good, men do have an obligation to act in accord with the natural law. What is done contrary to the natural law is necessarily lacking in some good, meaning that it is a sin that can incur God's punishment when it is committed. At the same time, it is important to distinguish what is done contrary to the natural law with what is done that goes beyond the limits of the natural law. The natural law works for the internal good of the created world, and it is only indirectly oriented to God beyond it as the ultimate good for all things that exist. Hence the proximate good as the end of the natural law is something that exists within the created world. Since virtue is to act in accord with the good, men must obey the natural law in this manner. But God also made men capable of knowing Him and loving Him so that they can attain to union with the Divine essence Itself in the state of beatitude. Thus God as the ultimate end for men is beyond the natural law. Yet since God gave men natural faculties to attain to this end, namely the rational intellect and free will, the movement of man to God is in accord with the natural law in some sense, but also moves men beyond the good possible to them from the natural law at the same time.

Since God gave men a rational intellect and free will, men can use these powers in order to understand the good that is in accord with the natural law and then to work to obtain it. It is evident that men have a rational intellect and free will for this purpose. The rational intellect of men can understand universals, which means that men can come to find the overall rules that they should follow in different cases for the sake of their own greatest possible good in each case. So while non-rational animals can know that they ought to seek food to satisfy themselves, they cannot know in any abstract way that the food that is sought and digested will keep them alive, or how the process of seeking their food is in accord with any greater good for them. The non-rational animal knows that this or that particular food gives it delight, and so it will seek out the food for that reason. But when men seek food, they can say that they need it to sustain life, and that it is good for them to continue to live. Hence a non-rational animal is aware of this life, this food, and what the food does for the animal body itself. Yet since men have a rational intellect, they can understand the abstract concepts of food, life, goodness, and so forth. This is what it means for the rational intellect to understand universal things. And the rational intellect also has the ability to contrast different things because it can make complex distinctions. This means that men can say whether this or that thing is either greater or lesser than some other thing. The concept of the good is abstracted from the different particular objects, and then the degree of goodness in the different objects is compared in order to see which of the objects is the greater. Since the good of itself is desirable, the man will be able to choose which of the different possible goods will give more delight in the end. It can be said that non-rational animals have some ability to contrast, but this is necessarily more limited than the capacity as it exists within men as rational beings.

The ability of the rational intellect of men to make these complex distinctions means that men also possess a free will that derives from the rational intellect. Men know things within the rational intellect. They can form an image in the rational intellect of the thing known, which image is called an idea. Once men have ideas about different things that they have contrasted with each other, they can choose one object over the other using the will that derives from the rational intellect. Since the will has more choices based on the greater number of distinctions made in the rational intellect, the will is necessarily a free will, where choice is the essence of freedom. This is the nature of human free will. While the will derives from the intellect, it also moves the intellect at the same time. So men can choose which objects about which to form ideas in the mind. When they choose to form an idea of one object over another, this is done through the power of the will. That the will derives from the intellect is an essential characteristic of the will as such, regardless of whether the subject has a rational or non-rational intellect. But since it takes a rational intellect to make more distinctions, a free will can only derive from the rational intellect, as the freedom of the will is based on choice, where the rational intellect can make more distinctions for the things that can be chosen in the end by the subject himself.

The free will of men necessarily means that men can do things contrary to what they do. It was already said that a choice for the sake of only one good is no choice at all. Choice means that there has to be more than one possibility for which the subject can act in the given case. And it is evident that men are capable of knowing good and evil. This was one of the consequences of the Fall. God allowed men to choose the evil over the good, thus bringing about the Fall, so that men could learn the difference between good and evil. Hence they could act for the sake of the good over the evil. This means that they become the proximate cause of the good that they did, with God as the ultimate cause thereof. Since they become the proximate cause of more of the good in this way, God can give them more of the good out of His perfect justice. Yet since men still retain their free will as part of their nature regardless of the Fall, they can use their free will for either good or evil. If they use their free will for the sake of the good, they act in accord with the different kinds of law that God has established for the sake of the greatest possible good for them as men. If they choose act for the sake of a lesser good, they defy the laws that God has established by His will. Now since God wills the greatest possible good for all things, and He made men to share His goodness with them, God seeks for men to act from a desire for the greatest possible good in every case. Thus the laws that God has established, which also work for the sake of the greatest possible good, carry with them an imperative quality for men. Men must act in accord with these laws in order for them to come into the greatest possible good in every case, and thus to act in accord with their nature as men in the way that God had made them in the first place. And if men fail to work for the sake of the greatest possible good in every case, they not only lose the good that they should have sought for themselves in the given case, they also can suffer from punishment from God for the way that they violated His will as expressed in the different kinds of laws that He established for the common good of mankind in particular and the rest of His creation in general.

It was said that God gave men their rational intellect and free will in order for them to freely work for the sake of the greatest possible good in the given case in accord with proper virtue. For men to work for the sake of the greatest possible good in this way means that they must first learn what is the good itself in the rational intellect. This is because the rational intellect is prior in idea to the free will that derives from it. So for men to work for the sake of the good means that they must know the good in the first place. Yet since the free will moves the rational intellect at the same time that the free will derives from it, it is possible for men to make errors in what they identify as the greatest possible good for which they ought to work in the given case. All of this concerns the conscience of men. The conscience is not a separate power in men apart from the rational intellect and the free will. It is the ability of these powers to properly discern the greatest possible good in the given case. Hence where God gave men their rational intellect and free will for the sake of their own greatest possible good, men make the possible good for themselves to be actual through the operation of the conscience. Men identify the greatest possible good in the rational intellect and then work for it by the free will that derives from the rational intellect. Thus the men become the proximate cause of the good that they do in this way not only by their ability to seek the good, but also by how they identify the good freely through the operation of the rational intellect. This operation is the essence of conscience.

But since men are still fallen beings, they can be in error about the nature of the greatest possible good that they ought to seek in accord with proper virtue. Hence a man may identify some lesser good as the greatest possible good in the given case. This means that to identify the lesser good in this way and then work for it above the other possible goods is objectively evil. Being is the same thing as goodness and evil is opposed to the good, meaning that evil is the lack of the being that can be present in the given case. Since things are defined by their ends, and the end of the act in this case is a lesser good, there is some being that is missing from the end thereof. Thus there is also some being missing from the act itself, as the act is the means to the end, and the end can only be obtained for what it is. So if being is goodness, and evil the lack of a possible being, to seek a lesser good over the greatest possible good is objectively evil.

Yet that the act is objectively evil does not mean at the same time that it is necessarily a sin. If the man truly did not know and could not have known that he chose a lesser good over the greatest possible good in the given case, no sin was committed. It is never just to hold a man to account for what he could not possibly know. Thus the man is excused from any sin through invincible ignorance. God out of His perfect justice does not punish men for things less rightly done if the men could not know what they did not know. And even men living in the fallen world can understand that men should not be punished for things that they did wrong where they could not have known enough to do otherwise. While the act might have materially come from the man in the given case, it did not formally derive from him because he did not intend the act as such. He intended to act for the sake of the greatest possible good in the given case, yet failed through no fault of his own. Hence he did well in a formal sense even though he did what was materially evil at the same time. He could not have known to do other than what he had done.

But the case is altogether different if the man acted for the sake of lesser good when he could have possibly known that the good that what he sought was a lesser good. In this case the man avoided knowing the greatest possible good because he had an inordinate desire for the lesser good that he eventually sought. His ignorance was the excuse for him to seek the lesser good over the greatest possible good in the given case. This is called vincible ignorance. And men can be held to account for avoiding the knowledge that they could have had for the sake of obtaining the greatest possible good in the given case. They still cannot be held to account for choosing the lesser good because they still did not know that they chose a lesser good. But they can be held to account for their ignorance of the greater good when they should have known about it.

There are two precepts that arise from the consideration of both invincible and vincible ignorance. The first is that men are still bound to obey their conscience even in the event that they incorrectly identify the greatest possible good in the given case. Thus it can be said that an erring conscience is still binding on the man. This means that even if the man acts for the sake of an objective lesser good, and so does what is materially evil, he is bound to act in this way insofar as he thinks that he acts for the sake of the greatest possible good. This is how the man formally acts with proper virtue even though he chooses a lesser good over the greatest possible good in the given case. His act is formally virtuous even though it is materially sinful. It is relatively good, meaning that he intended the greatest possible good at the time based on what he knew. And this is despite how the act is objectively evil, insofar as the good chosen was not the actual greatest possible good for the man in the given case.

The second precept is that men have an obligation to properly form their conscience. So while men cannot be held to account for choosing a lesser good over the greatest possible good in the given case, they still have a moral obligation to learn about the greatest possible good in order for them to work for the greatest possible good in accord with proper virtue. This means that men must use their rational intellect to know as much as is reasonably possible to them for their place in life. If the men know more, they can better find the greatest possible good for them, meaning that they can act for the greatest possible good in their free will and thus obtain to a greater delight in the end. Things exist for the sake of an end, and God gave men their rational intellect in order for them to find the good on their own. To find the good is itself virtuous, since finding the good is the first step that the men can make towards the possession of the good. And coming into the possession of the greatest possible good in the given case is the proper end of virtue. Men can work in this manner to come to God above all else, but also to work for the sake of the different created goods that are possible to them in life at the same time. The delight from the created good can show them more of God's own essential goodness, as God is the first cause of all things, and the effect always resembles the cause in some way. This is how God is the ultimate end for men in particular, in addition to being the ultimate end for all other created natures that exist.

Hence men have an obligation to form their conscience in accord with the desire for the objective greatest possible good in each case. They must do what is possible to them to find the truth in each case. When they properly find the truth for what it is, they can better tell apart the greatest possible good from any of the lesser goods, meaning that they can work for the greatest possible good in accord with proper virtue. And it can be said that a man's own conscience is the final authority under God to which he is bound. God is the ultimate judge of all things because He made all things to be what they are, and

He rules over the entire created world. So when God renders things to different created natures, He gives them all exactly what they deserve in accord with their nature. This is God's justice done to all things. Hence God will reward or punish all men in the end for the virtue or sin that they had in life, so that what they either get or lose will always be perfectly commensurate with what they deserve. This is an act of God's distributive justice. But since men cannot be expected to know what they do not know, and the man's own ability to act for the greatest possible good is limited by what he knows, men are bound to follow their conscience in every case. A man cannot be expected to submit to any authority contrary to what he actually knows and believes. This was said to mean that the man must still follow his conscience even when he may be objectively wrong but cannot know better than to believe or do what he does.

Yet while men are bound above all else to their own conscience, this does not mean that the role of conscience for men is absolutely autonomous. Men can bind themselves in accord with their conscience to submit to some other moral authority for the sake of their own greatest possible good. This is a necessary element of human life, considering that no man in the fallen world has an absolute monopoly on knowledge or judgment. Hence men might rightly recognize that some other men know better than they do in certain cases, and they can submit themselves to the other authority for the sake of their own good. When men are placed over other men in society, the men set over the other men can have more information about things because of their position over the other men. As they can take into account more information, they can use this information to better work for the sake of the greatest possible good in the given case. And other men can submit to them because these other men know better than they do. This is one of the ways that a man can work more efficiently for the sake of the greatest possible good in his own life.

That a man may submit to other men in good conscience does not at all mean that the man who submits abdicates his natural responsibility to work for the sake of the greatest possible good as he sees it. He does not allow the other man to take over for him and make the decisions that he ought to make for himself. If the man was to mindlessly follow the other men, he would indeed abdicate his responsibility to act for the sake of his own greatest possible good. God gave men their own rational intellect and free will so that they can individually work for the sake of the greatest possible good for them. Hence for a man to let other men blindly lead him in this way would be contrary not only to his own nature as a rational and intelligent being, it would also conflict with God's will at the same time, since God gave him the rational intellect and free will so that he can think for himself and find the greatest possible good in accord with what he knows. Thus it must be said that no man should ever choose to debase his nature by going along with an authority without thinking about what he does when he follows the authority. He can still follow the authority in the end, and this can still be for the sake of his own greater good, but he should do so intelligently. This means that he considers what the authority has told him to do, and provided that the authority's order makes sense to him in accord with what he knows, he can go along with the order. This way he makes the will of the authority to be his own will, which is the essence of obedience. An unthinking obedience means that a man leaves himself open to be abused by men who will take advantage of his trust and use his submission for their own good without regard for what is the good for him or other men in the given case.

When men choose to submit themselves to authorities in an intelligent manner, always considering the greater good for which they will work in accord with their obedience, they act in accord with proper virtue. This way the men can maintain their responsibility as individual men to work for the sake of their own greatest possible good while at the same time recognizing their own limitations in terms of what they know. Since they recognize their own limitations in terms of their knowledge, this can be a way for them to humble themselves before other men and above all before God. Humility means that the subject has an objective view of his own value. He does not think that he is either greater or lesser than he really is. So when men submit themselves to obey other men, they realize that the men whom they obey might know better than they do. Hence it makes sense that they trust the judgment of the other men and follow their orders for the sake of the greatest possible good for themselves in the given case. Thus the men who give the orders can work for the greater good of the men who obey them. And it is humility for the other men to submit to them in terms of obedience, meaning that they realize they do not know all of the things that they may need to know in life in order for them to find the greatest possible good. So when they recognize their limits in this manner, they do not abdicate their natural responsibility to use their rational intellect and free will for the sake of their own greatest possible good.

It can even be said that such an abdication in the name of a misguided obedience is actually the sin of sloth. Sloth means that the subject lacks the proper concern for the greatest possible good that he ought to seek in the given case. If a man gives up his own natural responsibility to find the greatest possible good by using his rational intellect, then he shows that he does not much care about the good that he should seek for himself. This is how this is the sin of sloth, which is a capital vice. So while true obedience is good for men, both in terms of humility and in their ability to find the greatest possible good, an unthinking obedience to any authority is contrary to proper virtue. It can even be said that an unthinking obedience to God is not good for men either. This does not mean that God could or would mislead men regarding the greatest possible good. Since all that God does is always good, God alone is perfectly trustworthy. But the men in the fallen state might ascribe the will of God either to demons or to their own imperfect desires. They might also see the work of God in things that they take to be signs when these things are not really signs at all. This is the sin of superstition or perhaps divination. Instead it is proper for men to test every spirit, so that men can avoid being misled regarding the good for them. This does not mean that they lack any trust in God. It only means that they are making sure that what they believe really is from God, and hence that they should follow it in obedience to the Divine will.

From what has been said, it is evident that while men are bound to other authorities under God for the sake of their own good, they are still bound to their conscience above all else. And in the event that an authority commands a man contrary to what he knows to be the truth or the good for him in the given case, there are ways that the man bound in obedience can disobey for the sake of his conscience. Now when a man submits to obey other men, it was said that this is done for the sake of his own good. The man realizes that the other men to whom he submits himself may know better than he does, meaning that he can better work for his own good under their direction than he can when he works on his own without their assistance.

But it might be that the man whom he obeys issues an order to which he is bound, but which does not appear to work for the sake of the greatest possible good. This can happen in one of two ways. First, the man who is bound to the order might see that it is mutually exclusive with some higher law to which men are bound. Hence the order might contradict the Divine law or the natural law. In which case the man is bound to disobey the human order because he has a higher responsibility to God compared to any created authority to whom he might also bind himself. In this case the man should risk punishment from the created authority rather than risk that God would punish him more if he was to obey the order that the human authority gave him. Second, the man who obeys might see that the order given does not work for the sake of the greatest possible good in accord with what he knows, but he also sees that the order does not conflict with any higher law. This means that the order is one of prudential judgment on the part of the one who issues the order. In this case, since the man has bound himself by obedience to the other man, he should recognize that the other man may have more information than he does about the greatest possible good in the given case. So the other man has a better possibility than he does to know the greatest possible good. This means that he ought to submit to the order all the same, since it might still be for the sake of the greatest possible good even if he cannot personally see how knowing what he is able to know at the time. And in the event that the order itself does not work for the sake of the greatest possible good, the culpability for the order itself lies with the one who gave it and not also with the men who were bound to obey him and execute the order itself. Since the virtue of obedience means to do the will of another, the responsibility for such an order lies with the one whose will it was that the order was done, and not with those who followed his lead and did the order as it was required of them. Part of the ability to rule over other men means that a man also accepts the moral responsibility on himself for anything that was less rightly done. And if the order less rightly given causes harm to more people, this is also his responsibility as well, meaning that he can justly be held to account for the harm that he caused when he gave the order. When a man does something wrong only in a private capacity, his punishment will be less than if he also bound other people to do something wrong, since the wrong that he did affected more people than just himself. This is why men in authority ought to be careful when they command the obedience of the men who are subject to them for the sake of their own good. They can suffer from a greater punishment in the end if the orders that they give to other men are less rightly given, so that they do not work as they ought to work for the sake of the greatest possible good in the given case.

Thus it is evident that men are bound to their conscience above all else, but that there are limits to their conscience at the same time, such as how men must work to properly form their conscience for the sake of finding the greatest possible good in the given case. Hence men cannot simply do whatever they want and claim that they acted in accord with their conscience in the given case. An erring conscience is still binding, but the risk of error must be mitigated by the necessity in each man of forming his conscience as much as possible in accord with what he knows to be the greatest possible good in the given case. Now it is also necessary to address the ways that conscience affects men as social beings. Man is a social animal, since one man by himself cannot work for the sake of his survival or his delight to the same degree as many men when they come together to work for the common good. Since men depend upon each other for the sake of the goods that they cannot obtain on their own, men must have some desire for the good of their fellow man as well as for their own good. This desire for the good of their fellow man can motivate them to work for the sake of the common good, so that all of the men, including them, may benefit from what results. So the good that men put out into society for their fellow man comes back to them in some manner when their fellow man works for their good as well. This is how a society of men is self-sufficient in a way that the same cannot be said for individual men.

    It is the case that men can use their social nature and their concern for the common good to move other men in good conscience for the sake of their own benefit. Now it was said that each man's free will is absolutely his own, so that one man cannot as it were take hold of the free will of another man and make that man's free will do as he pleases. As soon as the other man's free will is taken in control, it is no longer the other man's free will at all. Hence even if a man was to force the body of another man so that the other man seemed to do what the first man had willed, it is still the first man himself moving the other man's body, meaning that the movement does not come from the free will of the man who was moved. But while men cannot force the free will of other men, they can do things to help the other man act in their own free will for the sake of the greatest possible good in their own lives. Hence men can teach other men about the nature of the greatest possible good so that they can better work for the good itself by the free will that God gave them. It can even be said that this is a responsibility for men to instruct their fellow men for the sake of the good. This is one of the ways that a man can work for the good of his fellow man. And when he works for the good of his fellow man, his fellow man can better work for his good as well, since the men are bound to work together in the society that they formed with other men for the sake of the common good. Hence if more men are instructed in the nature of the good so that they can work for it in accord with their own free will, the whole society can become better in the end because of their virtue.

While men must use their individual free will for the sake of coming into the greatest possible good for them, this does not mean that the men who help them find the greatest possible good cannot use coercion in some ways when the good at stake is significant enough to warrant the coercion itself. A man cannot live in a human society and benefit the other men accordingly if he is allowed to do certain things that constitute grave sins, such as murder, rape, or theft. These things not only cause great bodily and moral harm to men, both the men who do them and the men who suffer from them, but they also undermine the proper functioning of the entire society. This is how the society as a whole can rightly coerce men by means of power or punishment to act in accord with proper virtue concerning these things. The use of coercion can compel the men within the society to see how these are serious matters for the whole society, and how God will also punish the men severely if they were to commit these criminal acts. Yet it belongs to the authorities who govern the human society to determine what constitutes certain criminal acts. Even if the society has made certain acts criminal, this still does not mean that the decision of the society itself to criminalize those acts overrides the primacy of conscience. There are times when corrupt societies may seek to outlaw virtuous acts in order to compel men to sin. In these cases as well, the men are still bound more to God through the natural law or the Divine law, meaning that the men in good conscience must disobey such laws and suffer the criminal punishment for the sake of the greater good that they can ultimately receive from God for their virtuous acts.

Thus it is evident that the societies in which men live properly allow some realm in which men can act freely according to their conscience. It was said that men can become better when they do things freely, since the good in that case more properly comes from them. As they become better, they can come into greater delight and a greater reward from God as the result of their acts. Hence the right of conscience, while not absolute, is a right that belongs to men as men. Now a right is defined as the establishment of some kind of equality for the sake of upholding the common good. As the purpose of a right is the common good, but the common good cannot be upheld in the same way in all cases, rights by their nature are circumstantial. But when the circumstances are themselves rooted in something that does not change, such as human nature, the right in this case is always present and must be upheld. The rights that are always present because they derive from unchanging circumstances are called natural rights. It is never just for any law to override the natural rights that men have while living in a society, since the origin of these rights is in the unchanging circumstances that apply to human nature.

But there is another kind of right other than a natural right. This is something that is based on changeable circumstances, meaning that it cannot always be upheld in each and every case for the men in different societies. These are called positive rights. So when it is good that there is some kind of equality established for the sake of the men in the society, but this same equality would not necessarily apply in some other case, then it is a positive right. In the event that the equality established by the law through the positive right does not work in the particular case for the sake of a greater good, then the positive right ceases to exist.

Now to better understand the nature of law as a rule that operates for the sake of the greatest possible good, it is necessary to consider the different natural rights that men have while living in society with other men. As the circumstances of these rights are always the same, it would not be proper for any human law to override the natural rights that belong to men. If such laws were to act in this manner, the laws would necessarily not work for the sake of the greatest possible good, meaning that men would be bound in proper conscience to disobey them for the sake of the actual good that is possible to them through this transgression. The greater good in accord with the natural right must override any human law. Men can be in error when they make laws in the fallen world, which means that such disobedience may be necessary for the men in the society. This way they can better act with proper virtue which the law should uphold in this as in other cases, as law and virtue both work for the sake of the greatest possible good.

The first and most important natural right that exists for men is life. Life is the ability of a thing to exert some control over its own existence. Hence when men are united in soul and body, so that the powers of the soul move the body for the sake of some good, the man himself is alive. Now it is necessary for human society to recognize the natural right of men to live. Men live in society so that they can work together for the sake of the common good. When there are more men living in the society, they can better assist the self-sufficiency of the society by their contributions to it. This is how it is better for there to be more people in a society. And since the greater number of men living in the society can help the society to be more self-sufficient, men in general have a natural right to continue to live. A right was said to be the establishment of some kind of equality among men for the sake of upholding the common good. So if more men in the society means that the society is better off in the end, men must have a natural right to live.

It may be supposed that certain kinds of men do not have the same right to live as other men. Some men may be of lesser intelligence than other men, meaning that their contribution to the society might be looked upon as lesser than that of someone with greater intelligence. Then there is also the case of men who are mentally or physically disabled, so that their disability keeps them from contributing to the society to the same degree as other men. It might also be supposed that the resources that such men require to live in the society are far more than what they can give back if they were allowed to live. But it must be remembered that the ways that men can contribute to the good of human society is not limited to the intellectual or material goods that they can produce under their own power.

For example, a man who is mentally disabled might retain the intelligence of a child for his entire adult life. The man cannot obtain greater knowledge as he gets older in the manner of someone who is not also disabled. This means that his contribution in either intellectual or material terms to his society will be more limited. Yet this does not mean that the man in this case contributes nothing at all, or that it does not make sense to allow him to live. His life and existence might bring delight to the men around him from the things that he is able to do. This is a different kind of contribution that such men can make in society. Although such a contribution cannot be quantitatively measured in the manner of other contributions, it would wrong to say that he does not contribute any good to his society. A similar circumstance might occur for someone who altogether lacks the use of the rational intellect and free will because of some disease or defect. The man might not even be able to communicate with others because of the degree of the disability. But this is still a possibility for the other men in the society who care for him to do some good on their own. They can learn to love the disabled man more selflessly when they care for him, since there is little to nothing that the disabled man can give back to the other men in exchange for the ways that they have to work to keep him alive. Hence it is not proper to say that the natural right to life is taken away in cases such as these, or even that the right to live is diminished compared to the case of a healthy man whose contributions to society are more readily apparent.

The same can be said for men who have physical disabilities as well that may prevent them from working more effectively for the sake of the greatest possible good. The man's own ability to do more of the good might be less compared to that of healthy men, but this does not mean that they make no contribution at all, or that their contribution does not benefit the society so that they still deserve to live. It is also the case that men who have either mental or physical disabilities might go onto make very great contributions to their society. There have been many men who have lived throughout human history in different societies that have made great contributions despite their adversities. In some cases they were even able to make their contributions because they were more determined as the result of having to overcome their adversity. Their suffering made them stronger, so that once they were able to live with their problems, they could go on to do greater things with the strength that they had gained from their experiences. So neither the mental nor the physical disabilities that are possible to men have to mean that the men are necessarily limited in their contributions in the first place. They might be able to contribute beyond the capacity of people who are healthier despite or even because of what they have suffered from their disability.

Similarly it must also be remembered that men cannot be judged based on the particular circumstances of their lives as a way to determine what they might contribute to society in the future. Hence if a man was born and raised in poverty, this does not mean that he will never be able to rise out of his poverty, or that his contributions to society will necessarily be minimal. Men must remember that there have been many men in the history of human society who have risen from lesser circumstances and went on to make great contributions that have benefitted all of mankind. While it may seem that being born or raised in less than auspicious circumstances might mean that men do not have the same right to live as men who come from better places, this is certainly not the case. Men who come from cases of poverty or abuse might have to do more to make a great contribution compared to the men who came from affluence, but they can still do great things for society and for mankind if they are given the opportunity.

Thus it should never be supposed that any individual man in society has a lesser right to live than other men because of circumstances that are beyond their control. The disabled or the poor have the same right to live as men who had more blessings in life. This is even the case if the men happen to be so disabled that they cannot even acknowledge the help that other men give to them. The society as a whole would be less without these people being allowed to live within it. It was said that it is never just to hold anyone or anything to account for something that did not come from the subject itself. So if a man did not will to suffer from his disability or the poverty in which he was raised, it would be gravely unjust to deny him the right to live for these things that happened to exist beyond his control.

This likewise raises the issue of abortion. It can be said that human life begins at the moment of conception. The two gametes that unite with each other are both alive, and they form a living organism. The organism thus created is necessarily alive, since what was not alive cannot be the cause of what is alive. And since the gametes came from the substance of the two different human bodies united in the sexual act, the organism that results is human as well. So the life of a human thus begins at the moment of conception. Now the unborn life lacks the use of free will, meaning that the human created at the moment of conception cannot be guilty of any personal sin or crime. There is the original sin in which all fallen men are conceived, but this is not a sin that the subject chose to commit, except in the case of the first men at the beginning of the human species. Hence the unborn human being cannot do anything wrong by which he would forfeit his right to live. For this reason it can be said that it is neither natural nor moral to ever kill an unborn child. This is totally contrary to the natural law and the good of the human society.

It might be supposed that if the child was conceived in terrible circumstances, such as through a rape or by a woman living in poverty, that she should be allowed to end the pregnancy. But this would be to hold the unborn child to account for something that the child could not have possibly done, and it is always unjust to hold men to account for things over which they had no control. At the same time, this would ignore how men cannot predict the future, meaning that they cannot say if a child conceived in terrible circumstances would either go on to benefit mankind in some significant way, or whether he will be a burden to his society. So it cannot be admitted that it is ever just for the child to be killed before he is born. To say that the child should be killed before birth just because the child exists in terrible circumstances would mean that the person who makes this claim assumes the same impossible knowledge of the future that was said to be the case for those who are disabled or who were born and raised in poverty. Men cannot make the claim with any certainty where such people will be in society if they are allowed to live. Hence it is proper that they recognize the natural right of all men to live in this manner.

But while men possess a natural right to live, this right to life is not so absolute that a society cannot execute men for their crimes. In such cases, the men forfeit their right to live by committing serious crimes, and the society executes them for the sake of the common good. This is altogether different from the other cases that were mentioned, since the other cases all involve men suffering from things that are beyond the control of their free will. The disabled or the poor are not in these states because they did something wrong, meaning that it is not proper to hold their state against them. The criminal chose to misuse his free will for the sake of committing a serious crime, meaning that he brought the punishment of death on himself for what he did. More will be said about this when treating the powers of the temporal state in making human laws.

Thus the right of men to live is a natural right. This is a right that is common to all men as such, and does not depend upon any changeable circumstances. While the concept of a right in itself is circumstantial, the circumstances in which innocent men have a right to live are always the same. Hence it is in accord with proper virtue that men do all that they can to uphold the rights of innocent men to live, both for their own good and for the good of human society. And it is always the case that any human laws made to govern the society must recognize the natural right to life for men. This right is also not compromised or diminished from one man to another. It is the case that some men do contribute more to their society or to mankind as a whole when compared to other men, meaning that the loss of such men is greater for some men than for others. But it is not under the ability of one man to determine the worth of another man. Each man must use his free will to the fullest extent of his ability for the sake of the good, so that he can come into the most delight for himself and also benefit the society in which he lives at the same time.

Since men are naturally social animals, men cannot survive on their own. They cannot have the mental and bodily rectitude consistent with good health in life if they are alone. And one of the most essential associations that men make in society is the family. This is a natural association of men based on blood relations. Now it is the case that men can do more of the good for those who are closer to them than those who are more remote from them. Since men are naturally closer to their family members because of the ties of blood, it makes sense to say that men have more of a moral obligation to work for the good of their family members than they do for other men. And from the closer blood relation that exists within families, it is usually the case that men also live in closer proximity to their family members than they do to others. This way men have more of an obligation to their families than they do to other men. Since it is good for men to live among their family members, the society in which the men live rightly recognizes this essential relation. If the society as a whole recognizes and protects the integrity of the whole family, then men can better work for their own good and the good of their family members, the latter because of their naturally close relation. This way the whole society can benefit more from the good that is done and the ways that the family members depend upon each other for their survival and delight.

It would be blatantly contrary to the rest of the society to attempt to ignore or undermine the integrity of families among men. Since the family is prior in idea to the whole society, insofar as the whole society is naturally composed of families, the family has rights of its own that the rest of the society cannot compromise. This would ultimately mean the destruction of the society in itself, as it would mean that one of the main constitutive elements of the whole society had been destroyed. If the family was to be destroyed, the rest of the society would eventually suffer collapse as well because of the way that the society failed to protect one of its main elements. Hence any good society, or indeed any association worthy of the name of a human society, has to recognize the role of individual families for the good of men in accord with human nature itself.

      Now since the family is one of the essential elements of human society, it makes sense that society itself would impose a structure on the family in order to protect the integrity thereof. This institution that works for the good of the family is called marriage. A man and a woman come together for the sake of the sexual act. Since the sexual act naturally results in children, and children are necessary for the society itself to continue, this means that the society as a whole has an interest in protecting the institution of marriage. It is within the context of marriage that a man and a woman can have children and raise them so that they can become properly functioning adults. As childhood is the most formidable time in the life of a man, it is critical for the man to become a healthy adult that he has a decent childhood in the context of the marriage of his parents. Since the parents came together in the sexual act to bring the child into being, they are ordinarily responsible for the raising of the child. And since the child comes from the bodies of the man and the woman united in the sexual act, the child as such belongs to his parents until he is old enough to support himself in the society. It is from this blood relation to the parents from whom he derived his being that he belongs to them more than to anyone else, including the society of which he is also a member. The society is based on the family, and the importance of the family is prior both in concept and in reality to that of the society.

It might be supposed that it is possible for a marriage to be formed between or among some other arrangement of individuals. Hence it might be said that it is possible for either two men or two women to be married, or even for more than two people to enter into a marriage. In the case of either two men or two women, there is no logical way that they can ever conceive a child. It is necessary for there to be gametes from both a man and a woman in order to make a child. Hence the only possible sexual act that can result in children is that of a man and a woman. All other sexual acts that are possible lack the element of procreation. Since procreation is the ultimate end for the sexual act itself, any sexual act lacking in the possibility of procreation is inherently missing a necessary element, meaning that it is lacking in due rectitude. And this was already given as the definition of a sin. While it is possible for people to conceivably derive some other purpose from the sexual act, the ultimate purpose of the act is procreation. As marriage exists for the sake of the man and woman being able to engage in the sexual act and to raise the children who are conceived in the sexual act, marriage is only possible between a man and a woman.

It might also be said that if it is possible for barren couples to wed, it should also be possible for two men or two women to do the same. The barren couple also cannot procreate, which would seem to mean that there is no difference between them and these other couples. But this cannot be said. If a man and woman are barren but still retain the sexual organs of their bodies, it is still logically possible that they can become fertile and conceive a child. It is not that some of the parts were missing from the pairing, it is only that one or both of the parts do not operate in the way that they should. Since it is possible for a barren couple to become fertile, it is still logically possible for them to form a valid marriage. The same cannot be said for either two men or two women because they have the same parts, meaning that some parts that need to be present for procreation are inherently lacking in their pairing. So the case of a barren couple being married is necessarily different from that of either two men or two women. Yet if a man or a woman is altogether lacking in the sexual organs, then it is not possible for a valid marriage to be formed between the two of them. This means that there is no way that the sexual act as the marital debt can be paid. But it was said that marriage exists for the sake of the sexual act and the children who were conceived in the act itself. If there is no way to pay the marital debt and thus conceive a child, then there is no way that a valid marriage can ever be formed. If the end for which something exists is removed, so is the means to the end, since the means exists for the sake of the end. As sex and procreation are the end of marriage, there can be no marriage at all where these things are not logically possible, not even in the event that the pairing is between a man and a woman.

There is also the possibility that a marriage can be formed in the context of more than just one man and one woman. It is evident that a man or a woman can engage in sex with many different other people of the opposite sex at the same time. There is no natural limit to the ability of either the man or the woman to restrict themselves to just one other person, even if the other person is of the opposite sex. And it is evident that there have been many different societies throughout human history where either bigamy or polygamy was considered acceptable. But while there is no natural reason why such unions cannot be formed, it makes sense for the sake of social order that men and women only form monogamous relationships. For example, if a man is married to many different women at the same time, and he has children with all of them, he will have less time and ability to devote himself to the good of either his wives or his children. And men ought to give a decent amount of attention to their wives and children for the sake of their marriage and the health of the children that they conceived. If there are many wives, and probably also many children from the different wives, then someone will likely be neglected because there are so many people to whom he is simultaneously responsible in some manner. The man would also have to work to support the wives and children, which would be more difficult because of their much greater numbers. Hence for the sake of order in the family and in the society as a whole, it can be said that monogamous marriages necessarily work more for the sake of the greatest possible good. So if any bigamous or polygamous relations are to be formed, it is necessarily the case that only the first such marriage is valid, since the others do not work in the same way and to the same degree for the sake of the greatest possible good.

Since the family is one of the natural and most essential associations of men that exist in human society, it is necessary that the whole society works through the laws that it produces to uphold the integrity of the family. And while marriage itself is not a natural institution, in the sense that it organically occurs among men, it is still natural in the sense that it conduces to the well-being of men and women and the children that they conceive in the sexual act. As this is how the society itself can continue, it is proper that there is an institution to guard the integrity of the family, even if this institution is itself a human creation. While marriage is itself a human creation, the different aspects of the marriage that have been explained are necessary for it to be what it is. A marriage that is formed in some other way besides one man and one woman, or a marriage that is inherently closed to procreation, does not meet the definition of a marriage. Hence any such unions, whatever their nature or the ways that men in society may consent to their existence, are invalid. They are not marriages in any degree because they do not meet the essential characteristics that are part of the definition of a marriage.

It also conduces to the marriage that the man and the woman joined together remain with each other for life. This way they can work together for the good of their children when the children are still young, and their union can provide stability for the children as they become adults. They can also pass on their material wealth to their children as an inheritance when they die. This way they can benefit the children even when the children are adults and are capable of supporting themselves. But the additional wealth obtained through the inheritance means that the children can be better off by having more material goods to their name. This can help them to maintain the stability of their condition in life, and to also help the whole society, so that the men in the society are better guarded against any kind of monetary difficulty that they might have to experience. This is how it conduces to the greater good that the man and woman remain married for the rest of their lives, even as their children are grown and capable of supporting themselves.

The primary duty of the man and woman in marriage is to raise their children so that they can become decent functioning adults. But it can also be said that the man and woman within the marriage have duties to each other as well for the common good of the whole family. Hence it is the natural role of the man to support his wife and children so that the family has the material wealth that it needs to survive. At the same time, it is the duty of the wife to maintain the household that her husband works to support. And while both the husband and the wife have roles to play in the raising of the children, their roles are necessarily different. A man cannot do what a woman can do for her children, nor can she do what he can do for them at the same time. But since the woman is in charge of maintaining the home, it is proper to her to take the more involved role in the lives of the children while they are still young. The man still has an integral role to play by the way that he financially supports the family and rules over the household at the same time. In this way they both have different and complementary roles to play for the common good. In the same way that the different parts of an animal body all work together for the sake of the whole, the man and woman in the marriage work with each other in different ways to maintain the household for themselves and for their children.

Aside from the children, the man and woman in marriage owe each other more goods in particular for their own sake. The man must protect and support his wife so that she has the various material goods that she needs to run the household. And the woman has the obligation to love and obey her husband so that she can sustain him in his efforts. This way they can work together so that the two of them are self-sufficient in a way that is not possible to either of them if they were alone. This is one of the ways that the family can be considered a microcosm of the larger society, since these different parts work for some degree of self-sufficiency that is not possible for men when they are alone.

The children in the household have a more limited role to play for the good of the whole, because they lack the use of reason in their earliest years and only later can work more for the sake of their own good. But since they naturally depend upon their parents for the sake of their own good, they have a duty to obey the parents when the parents give them orders. Just as the man who is set over other in men society has more knowledge of what needs to be done for the good of the whole society, the parents can use their better knowledge and their position set over their children to work for the good of the children. Since the children generally do not know better or even as well as the parents, the children should obey the parents as much as they can. And for the way that the parents supported the children when the children were young, the children can work to support their parents when the parents are old and can no longer survive on their own. This is one of the ways that the children can pay back to their parents for the good that the parents did for them when the children were still young. The children received their lives from their parents, and while they cannot give back to the parents a good that is equal to what they had received, they can still act with gratitude for the way that they received their lives from their parents along with the other good things that the parents did for them at different times throughout their lives.

Hence it can be said that the family is formed and maintained through reciprocal relations among the different members. The husband, the wife, and the children all have different goods that they deserve from the other family members, and in turn contribute some good back to the family as a whole. This is all done in accord with justice, which is to give to all things what they deserve as what they are. This is a natural justice that exists in the created world, since the relation among the different family members is in accord with their nature as men.

Now since the children come from their parents, and so are part of them in a sense, the parents exercise a natural and immediate dominion over their children. This is especially the case when the children are young and still unable to support themselves. And one of the ways that the parents can work for the good of their children is to protect the children from any outside negative influences in the society itself that may cause either mental or bodily harm to the children. As the parents are closest to their own children when compared to the other men in the society, they can best determine what is in the best interest of the children when they are young. This way they can properly shield them from any harm or corruption, which is especially necessary given the way that youth is the most formidable time in the life of men. The negative experiences that may damage the child can last for the rest of his life, even after he has become an adult, meaning that it is especially important that children are protected by their parents from any outside harm. And the natural love that the parents ought to have for their children as being part of them in a sense means that they are the ones properly charged with caring for them in this way. The right of the parents to care for their children is a natural right based on how the children came from the parents and are part of them. For the men to protect their children is an extension of the way that men rightly protect their own bodies from any harm or unwanted experiences.

But it may be the case that the parents of the children do not act as they should for the sake of the good of the children. They might be negligent or abusive in the way that they treat their children, so that the children do not receive from the parents the good that is due to them in order for them to become functioning adults in society. In such cases it is proper for the rest of the society to intervene to take away the children for their own good, even though this means that the right of the parents to raise their children is overridden. The parents have a natural right to raise their own children and to protect them from any outside harm that may come to them from the rest of the society. Hence the good of the children is the reason that the parents exercise this dominion. But if the parents abuse their dominion over their children so that the children are seriously mistreated, then the good for the children as the end thereof can be obtained by taking the children away from the parents. The dominion of the parents over the children is for the good of the children, meaning it relates to that good as the means to the end. If the end is not met, there is no reason for the means. This is how other men in the society can intervene for the good of the children in order to protect them from abuse or neglect. This way the children can be raised in a proper home so that they can become properly functioning moral adults.

In the same way that the society as a whole can punish men for the sake of the common good, it can be said that the parents can punish their children for the good of the family or even for the good of the children themselves. If a child defies the order that his parents gave him, the parent can punish the child in some way so that the child can better understand right and wrong. The child can realize that there are consequences to his acts, and that he will suffer all the more if he fails to act for the sake of the greater good in the way that he was instructed. The kinds of punishments that children receive for their disobedience can vary based on the age of the child or the nature of the disobedience. A lesser offense from a child who is ordinarily more obedient can warrant a lesser punishment while a more disobedient child who committed a much greater offense can be punished more severely. This is as much an act of justice as it is for the society as a whole to punish adults for their crimes or offenses. It is also the case that physical punishment can be used for children as well, since the pain incurred by the punishment may make it easier for the children to understand that they should not disobey in the way that they did. As with the other kinds of punishments, the severity thereof must be measured for the degree of the offense. The ability of the child to endure the punishment must also be considered as well. A younger and smaller child would suffer worse from a particular punishment than one who is older and stronger. In which case even if the offense itself is greater from the younger and smaller child, a punishment of a lesser degree may be necessary to make it clear that he should not have done what he did. These are all different criteria to be considered when the parent imposes a punishment on the child for the child being disobedient to the parent's order.

From what has been established, it is clear that the family is the most important of the different elements that form in human society, and that the society itself should do all that it can to uphold the integrity of the family. The institution of marriage should be guarded against any abuse, and the parents of the children conceived and born within the context of the marriage should do all that they can so that the children can become functioning adults. The parents have a natural right to raise their children, to determine what is in their best interest, to protect them from harm that may come from other men in the society, and to teach them discipline so that they can learn in their own lives to work for the sake of the greater good. Once the children have become adults who are capable of working effectively for the sake of their own greatest possible good, they can benefit the society according to their particular abilities. This allows the society to continue. Since the continuation of the society itself, as well as its thriving, depend upon the good of the marriage and the family, the rest of the society should do all that it can to promote these related institutions. A society that is not just and does not work for the good of the family cannot be expected to survive or to work for the good in any degree for its members. Such a society has contradicted the most basic precepts of the natural law, and will inevitably come upon its own decline and destruction.

While the family is the most essential institution in human society, and the one upon which the society itself depends more than any other, it is also necessary for men in society to associate with other men on their own terms. One of the ways that this is possible is with friendship. While two or more friends might not be related to each other, they can still learn to care about each other in the same way that they are concerned for their own good. A friendship is when two or more men desire the good for the other in the same way that they desire the good for their own sake. And this desire for the good is called love. Hence friendship is a mutual bond of love between or among different people. And it is necessarily the case that there is reciprocity in the friendship. A man cannot be friends with someone who is not friends with him in return. He can still love someone who does not love him, but he cannot be friends with him unless the man also considers him to be a friend at the same time. Now when two or more men desire the greatest possible good for each other in friendship, then they will work for the good of the other for his own sake. This means that each man does more for the other men in the society for the sake of the greater good, so that the society as a whole can benefit all the more. This is how a friend is a second self.

As the society has a stake in seeing that men are able to form friendships, it is proper for the society to allow or encourage such relations among men. And it was said that a right takes place for the sake of some good. Since friendships among men work for the sake of the greater good for the men and the society as a whole, men have a right to associate with each other in this manner. It would be dangerous to the society to discourage such relations, because this could have the effect of increasing discord among men in the society, which can lead to social fracture.

Men can make other associations with each other as well. Friendship is formed over a mutual desire for the good of the other for his own sake. But it is the case that the good that men desire when they associate with each other can take different forms. If the men desire the good of the other for his own sake, this is virtuous friendship. This was the kind of friendship that was already explained. But there can be other kinds of friendship as well. If men associate with each other for the sake of some other good that they want, this is useful friendship. And if men associate with each other because they give each other delight without there being any meaningful concern for the good of the other, this is pleasant friendship. These other kinds of friendship differ from the virtuous friendship because they have the good of oneself as the proper end thereof rather than the good of the other. This does not mean that these other kinds of friendship are evil or that they should not take place, but it does mean that they are not lasting in the same manner as virtuous friendship. If the use or the pleasure of the other friendships was to disappear, then the friendship itself will come to an end. But since the end of virtuous friendship is the mutual desire for the good of the other, the friendship will endure as long as both of the men are alive to will the good for the other in the same way that they will the good for themselves.

Now the useful friendships in particular can be the basis for other associations that men can form in society for the sake of their own good and for the common good of the whole society. Hence if men find themselves working in the same field or profession, they can come together to uphold the good of the profession itself. This is how men can form guilds, which are voluntary associations of men working in the same field who come together to work for their common good. And the men who are in one guild can also work together with the men of other guilds at the same time, so that each guild can provide the other with some necessity in order for all of them to work more effectively in their respective fields or professions. This can be an example of a useful friendship because the men in the guilds all have the interest in upholding the good of the field or profession itself. So it makes sense that they would all work for the sake of their good together. And since they all know, as members of the field or profession, what needs to be done for the good of the same, they can work better for the rest of the society who depends upon their work for its own good. This is how the society itself can be considered a society of other societies. But since the good for which the men work together is that of the field or profession, their association can be called a useful friendship. Virtuous friendships might develop among them at the same time, and these can better help the society itself to grow closer together as well in the ways that were said.

The men working together in the society in the context of guilds or other associations means that they all join together for the sake of their own material good. Men need to work for the sake of their survival. Since men live together in society with other men, it makes sense that they would all contribute some good to the other men in the society in order to get back some good from them. As men all have different talents, some men can work in one way to provide a good for the other men that the other men cannot provide for themselves, while the other men can do the same for them. This was said to be how the society itself is self-sufficient. Now since men need material goods in order for them to survive and have some reasonable degree of delight in life, it can be said that the ability of a man to materially support himself by his work is a natural right. A right was said to be the establishment of some equality for the sake of upholding the greatest possible good in the given case. And a natural right is a right that is based on circumstances that do not change. Since men all have different abilities to work for their survival, the ability of a man to work to support himself by his labor is in his own best interest, and by extension, that of the whole society in whose support he assists by his labor. To withhold from a man the means of his ability to support himself is contrary to the natural law and to the man's own natural right.

Yet at the same time, it is the case that some men are impeded by either mental or bodily defect from being able to materially support themselves. This means that they cannot get the material goods that they need to live. Now it was already said that a man's natural right to live cannot be taken away from him even if he is unable to support himself in the society. While the man may not be able to get the material goods on his own in order to support himself, he can still contribute to the society in other ways. These ways may not result in the acquisition of material goods for his survival, but this does not preclude him from giving something back to the society. Since the men in such a position cannot support themselves, it makes sense that other men in the society will use their own labor to support them. This is the only way that the society itself can respond with proper virtue to the man unable to support himself, since the society cannot ignore that the man still retains his natural right to live. And insofar as the man unable to support himself can pay back to the other men in non-material ways, there is some justice in the way that the rest of the men within the society work for his support. Even if he responds with gratitude to the other men, since he can give no more to them, this is a way for him to give back some non-material good to the rest of the men in the society who support him.

That there is an obligation for the society to support the men who are unable to work for their own material support does not have to mean that this burden will necessarily fall with the temporal state that governs the society as a whole. It is proper for there to be private associations that can work to support these men. Hence if a man was a loyal and devoted member of a guild, and worked many years in the service of his field, but then he can no longer support himself due to some mental or bodily infirmity, the rest of the guild for whom he worked can contribute to his support and the support of his family. So while he paid back into the system by his years of work as a member of the guild, the other men can give back to him in his time of need. And if there is a man who is disabled and was never able to work at all, but he has family who are members of a particular guild, the guild can do the same for the disabled man as recompense to the family for the devoted work of the family's guild members. It is not a foregone conclusion that the temporal state as a whole has to support those unable to work. If this can be handled in some way by private associations, it can work better than requiring the entire temporal state to support the disabled men through its resources. Only if there is no other way to support the disabled should the temporal state be required to provide any support.

Since men have a natural right to work for the material goods that they need in order for them to survive, it can be said that they also have a natural right to exclusively possess the goods that they have procured for themselves in this way. This means that men have a natural right to own private property and to use that property both for their own advancement and for that of the people around them. If the natural right of men to earn their own private property and to use it as they please is recognized by the society itself, then the society can benefit all the more. Men will do more to work for the good of society if they have a clear stake in the outcome. So if men have private property as the result of the works that they did for their survival and their delight, they will make more of an effort to serve the society to get back some goods in exchange for their labor. This is also an essential function of justice in human society. If men give up the good when they work so that the society can benefit from their efforts, it is proper that they receive something in return for the good that they did. So private property not only benefits the whole society, it is also part of justice for the society to allow men to possess things exclusively in this manner.

    It might be supposed that it would work better for a society not to have private property because of the conflicts that arise among men over ownership of the property. The men who have no private property or very little private property will always want more, and they might even be moved to take by force from those who have more than they do. While this is the case, the common ownership of property in a human society would mean that men have little or no incentive to work to support the whole society. They will try to rely other men who will work to do the same. Yet if all of the men rely on the other men for the sake of material property, and no one works, then the society itself cannot survive. The men in the society would all suffer from privations and might even starve because no one works for to produce any material goods. The only way that such a society might be perceived to work is if the men were forced to produce the material goods. This would contradict another natural right of men, which is their free will to do as they please for themselves and for others within reasonable limits. So the negation of private property by common ownership would override one natural right, and it could only be upheld by overriding another natural right. Since the natural rights of men exist for the sake of upholding the common good, this cannot be done. And because the ownership of private property is a natural right rather than a positive right, it is always the case that a society must recognize the right of private property among men for the sake of their own good. This does not differ among time and place in terms of the positive rights that are possible to men.

Yet since men are allowed to earn and to own private property as the result of the work that they do for the common good of the society, it is perhaps inevitable that some men will be able to earn more material goods for the work that they do in the society. Other men will find their work more valuable in some way compared to the work of other men, meaning that they will have more material goods in the end than the other men. This is an inevitable part of any society, particularly one that allows men to act more freely for the sake of their own survival and delight. That the distribution of the material goods is not equal for all men is not necessarily evil. It is a natural part of any human society. But at the same time, it is the task of the society through its laws to make sure that the system itself by which material goods are allocated is as just as possible for the work that men are willing to do in the society. So if a man is willing to work for a reasonable amount of time and to make a decent effort for the sake of some good, he should in turn receive the amount of material goods that he needs to sustain himself in life. The society itself should do what is possible to make sure that men do not work great amounts while still not being able to survive. It would be unjust in principle for the society itself to allow men to suffer from the lack of necessary material goods while they were still working to support themselves.

The production and allocation of material goods is the concern of economics. And it is evident that economics is governed by laws that should not be ignored. To ignore the ways that a market operates would have gravely negative effects on the people in the society itself. But while the freedom of commerce in the marketplace is to be upheld, it is often necessary for the temporal state to enact certain laws to allow for the free and reasonably equitable distribution of the material goods. For example, if one man's material goods are in higher demand than that of other men, there is a possibility that he will become much richer than they are. This in itself does not have to be evil or negative for the society. But the man might use his abilities within the market to destroy any competition. Then once he is the only provider for the particular kind of material goods that he produces, he can unnecessarily increase the prices on them to add to his material wealth. Thus he will exploit the dependence of the consumers on his ability to control the market within his society. If something of this nature was to occur, it would be expedient for the temporal state to divide his business among other men in order to restore some reasonable competition.

It is also the case that the existence of guilds or other such associations could possibly prevent one man or his business from entirely taking over the market for the material goods that he produces. If the men in the guild work together for their common benefit, then the guild itself can work to maintain reasonable competition among the different men in the guild so that one or more of the different individual men does not become too powerful over the market for the goods that the guild produces. And if the guild itself, as a private association of men who all work in the same field, can regulate the marketplace for the particular kind of material goods produced, then there is no need for the temporal state to involve itself at all with the way that the guild operates in the marketplace. This means that the guild members themselves, as the men who know what needs to be done with these material goods and what the marketplace is like for those goods, can keep things running properly for the good of all of the men in the guild. Thus the restraints of this nature on the competition in the marketplace can maintain the competition within a reasonable field, so that one man or his business working in the field does not overtake the market itself and destroy all of the competition in the field itself.

Hence it is necessary that there are some regulations over the marketplace in order to uphold the reasonable free competition that takes place within that context. And if there is a guild or some other regulatory association to manage the market affairs for the good of all of the men in the guild itself, then one man will not be able to destroy the business of the other men also in the guild at the same time. If they are all in the same guild, for one of the men to harm the business of the other men to an excessive degree would mean that he also hurt himself at the same time, since this kind of competition would undermine the guild of which he is also a member. He would hurt himself if he tried to completely destroy the business of the other men within the guild itself. And if any of the men in the guild were to try to act in this way, the guild itself can stop such an event from taking place. And if the guild is able to thrive in this manner, the rest of the society can benefit at the same time from the material goods produced by the guild members.

It is similarly possible that the goods produced in a guild are not so much material goods in the sense of a physical item that men can use for the sake of some other good, but are more abstract concepts as well. Thus men can form guilds for the sake of providing services to the men in the society itself, such as education. It is logical enough that men who work in the same field or profession would know best what needs to be done in the field or profession for the good of the whole and for the benefit that the guild provides to the society in general. This means that there is potentially no real limit that is possible to the private associations that men can develop in order to manage the different parts of the society itself. And the different associations that the men have formed can work to provide services in exchange for the money that they earned. Hence they both give and get back some good for what took place, which is the natural order of justice.

Since economic matters are being considered, it is necessary to add that while men can exchange material goods or services for money, it is never permissible for men to try to use money itself for the sake of making more money. This takes place in the form of usury, which is to charge any interest on the money that is lent. Men can lend money to other men for the good of the other men, but it is never permissible for the lender to ask for more money back than the money that he lent in the first place. Justice means that a thing gets the equal of what it deserves as what it is. Hence if a man lends money to another man, all that is necessary for justice to be done is that the borrower give back the same amount of money he received. This is an example of commutative justice between the lender and the borrower. If the lender was to charge more money to use the money that he lent, this would mean that he charged twice for the same thing. Money as such has no inherent value of its own, since it is a neutral state of material value. Thus the money was lent so that it could be used for something else. Then to charge for the use of the money in the form of interest is to charge twice for the same thing, which is excessive. This is why it is never acceptable for a man to lend money at interest. It is contrary to commutative justice as the rule that governs the transaction. So if a society is to uphold the material good of its members, then it is necessarily the case that usury is never allowed. To allow men to lend money at interest would violate one of the natural laws that govern the use and allocation of material goods.

So while men have a natural right to work for the sake of their own material goods, and to make money as the means to acquire what they need in order for them to survive, it is never the case that men can make money from money itself in the form of usury, since this is contrary to the proper order of commutative justice that governs lending and borrowing among men. It is also the case that men have a natural right to be compensated if they lost some material good because of something less rightly done by someone else. This does not have to mean that the man who suffered from the loss of a material good was necessarily the victim of a crime. It belongs to the temporal state that governs the society to decide whether such injurious acts ought to be made crimes. But if a man does something that results in another man losing a good, it is right and proper that the man who caused the loss compensate the other man for the loss itself. If it was not for the sake of the man who acted negligently or recklessly, the other man would not have lost the good. Hence that man should reimburse the other man for the good itself. And if there is any conflict about the amount or the form of reimbursement, then the temporal state or even a private agency can settle the dispute between the men. There is no reason why the man who suffered the injury should have to go without the good itself through no fault of his own, especially when the loss of the good was the result of someone else doing what should never have been done.

      Now there are some cases when the loss of a possible good is not the result of a man acting either negligently or recklessly. Sometimes the man who suffered the loss might believe that the loss was the work of the other man, but the other man did not do anything that a reasonable man in the given case would be expected to do in order to prevent any injury. In which case the man who suffered the loss can be entitled to some compensation, but it does not have to come from the man whom he thought was at fault. If the other man can prove that he did nothing wrong, then he does not have to reimburse the man for the way that the man had suffered. These are the different things that private law can adjudicate among men. The nature of the fault or any compensation can be governed by the laws of the temporal state or some other governing association in order to make sure that justice is done for the men involved in the dispute itself.

These are the different ways that men can acquire material property for the sake of their survival and their delight in life. And it was said that the acquisition and ownership of material property are natural rights for men. It has also been said that men possess other natural rights as well, such as the right to life and the right to associate with other men in different ways for the sake of the common good. Of the associations that men can form for the sake of their own good and that of the whole society, the most important association is that of the family. Since the children in the family come from the bodies of their parents, the parents have certain rights over the children for the good of the children. The children also have certain rights as well. Both the parents and the children are bound to each other in the family by certain rights on the one hand and by obligations on the other. It is proper for the rest of the society to recognize and respect these things for the good of all of the men in the society, since a human society in general cannot exist without the preservation of the family. Thus the family itself, as well as other human associations, all have certain rights insofar as their existence and continuance is for the common good of the whole society, where the common good is the purpose for which these rights exist.

So far only natural rights have been considered. But it is also the case that there are positive rights as well that are possible to men in society. Natural rights are based in circumstances that never change, while positive rights are based on circumstances that may vary from one time and place to another. And it is proper that the temporal state that governs the human society can recognize some of these rights as well provided that the circumstances make it possible. But it was said that a right in general is the establishment of some kind of equality for the sake of upholding the common good. Thus the circumstances in which the common good may be upheld determine whether there is a right in the first place. Since the natural rights are based on circumstances that never change, the particular case does not have the same role in those cases that it does in other cases where the right itself may differ from one place to another. Hence it is not as easy to make general rules for all men concerning positive rights. The temporal state might decide in one place or another to recognize certain positive rights because the recognition of the right works out for the better in the end for the men in the society. But if it does not work out as well, it is not a right at all and the temporal state is under no obligation to recognize it. It may even be that a positive right is recognized in one temporal state at a given time but not at another. This depends upon the ways that the conditions within the society might have changed from one time to another.

Yet while it is difficult to establish general rules for positive rights beyond the principles that have been established here, it is still possible to speak of certain things that a human society may see as a positive right. For example, men need some kind of housing in order for them to survive. This means that the temporal state may consider housing as a particular material good for men that it ought to recognize as a positive right. This means that the temporal state can do what is reasonably possible to make sure that as many men as possible have homes that they own. And when the men own their own homes, they have a personal stake in the society through the home itself that they seek to maintain for their own good and that of their family. This means that they have more of a reason to work more diligently in what they do for the society, because if the rest of the society was to collapse, their own stake in the society through their home ownership would also be lost at the same time. This is one of the ways that a society can recognize a positive right among men for the sake of the common good.

Another positive right that is possible to men in human society is the right to defend oneself according to particular means. The right of self-defense in general is a natural right. This is the same for all men as such regardless of any other circumstances. Men are bound to work more for their own good than they work for the good of others, since their own good is more immediate to them and thus relatively greater than the good for other men. And if a man works to protect his own good within reasonable limits, he can better serve the rest of the society as well. The man cannot work as much for the good of the rest of the society if his own good is not upheld at the same time. The man would have to focus more on his own good than on the good of the rest of the society or even just the other men around him. Since it is always good for the society in this way for a man to defend himself against harm, this is a natural right. No temporal state can ever justly deprive a man of his natural right to self-defense, because doing so would only undermine the greater good and the very order that exists in the society itself.

But there are many different ways in which a man can exercise self-defense. Hence the temporal state can recognize that a man ought to have access to certain weapons for the sake of his protection. The use of such weapons can be necessary in some cases for men to defend themselves and those close to them in accord with their natural rights, and also to deter the other men from trying to harm them in the first place. So if the temporal state decides that the benefits of men having these weapons outweighs the risks that the weapons will be used in immoral ways, then the possession or use of such weapons can be considered a positive right. It may even be the case that the recognition of the positive right to use certain weapons for self-defense makes possible the natural right of self-defense in general, so that the natural right of self-defense in the circumstances of the human society is only reasonably possible by protecting the positive right to this or that weapon for that purpose. Much depends in such cases on the particular circumstances, but this is at least plausible for some societies in certain times and places.

The temporal state might decide that men have a positive right to a decent education in a field or profession of their choice. Perhaps the means of some men in the society to obtain an education are limited, such as if those men live in poverty and cannot fund the costs of an education in one or another field or profession. In which case the temporal state can organize some particular means for men in poverty to get an education in the hope that they might rise out of their state and contribute something significant to the rest of the society. If the men have great ability but are limited by their financial means at the same time, then either the temporal state itself or some kind of private association can fund the education for the poor. This can have the effect of lifting many men out of poverty so that they can make greater contributions to the rest of the society in exchange for being able to use their abilities to the fullest. Since the society can benefit in this manner, this can be considered a positive right. It may not be the case that there is a need in some societies for men to receive much of a formal education, meaning that this does not have to be a natural right. It can benefit the society in some cases if more men are educated, but the society itself on the other hand might have a greater demand for unskilled labor, meaning that an education would not be in the best interest of all of the men involved.

There is also the possibility that a formal education may send too many men into certain fields or professions while the others do not have the numbers of men that they need to adequately serve the society itself. This is a case where the different guilds in the society can work among themselves to see that some fields or professions receive the men they need while others do not have too many men. This can avoid economic problems for the society as a whole. For example, if there are too many men in one field, there will not be enough of a demand for the goods or services in that field for all of the men to have a decent amount of work in order for them to survive. In which case all of the men in the field will suffer from low wages and possibly even poverty because the demand for the goods or services was not as much as the supply of the men able to provide those goods and services to the society. Too many lawyers and not enough legal cases in the society can mean that all of the lawyers will suffer from lack of work and lower income.

So while an education can be considered an important positive right for men in society, it is at the same time not a natural right. And the individual men in the society also ought to consider for their own benefit the nature of supply and demand concerning goods and services so that none of the different fields or professions become too overloaded with people while others suffer from a lack of people to provide the goods or services. Either way, these two different circumstances will put a strain on the whole society, which can undermine the common good. And the common good for the whole society is the proper end of all rights, as it was said.

It might be considered whether access to medical care is considered a positive right by the temporal state. Men ought to have access to medical care so that they can sustain their lives and the quality thereof. This indeed relates to the nature of men as such, meaning that it would seem to approach being a natural right. But while it is always good for all men to have adequate medical care, this does not mean that men necessarily should have equal access to the medical care in every case. In theory, it is best that the poor or the needy have the same access to medical care for their issues as what is given to the wealthy. Yet if it is the case that the medical care provided to men for their issues is given to all men at the same time, it might not be possible for the supply of the goods and services in the medical profession to give all of the men all of the goods that they need. This would mean that rather than some men receiving adequate medical care while other men do not receive the same, all of the men in general would receive poor quality care because of the way that the entire profession has been overburdened by demand. This does not mean that the poor or the needy are less deserving of medical care compared to those who have more money. It is simply the reality that an equal amount of goods and services to all people would not be possible or sustainable for any reasonable amount of time. While it is inherently unjust that some receive better care or more care than others who also need care at the same time, it is better that some good is done for some people rather than that no good is done for all of them. While such a system does contain a grave injustice, it cannot be said at the same time that this is the result of any evil will on the part of any individual men or even all of society. A society that cannot give medical care equally to all of those who need it does not have to lack some concern for the good of the men in the society. The problem is that there are never enough resources to give everyone what they truly deserve for the sake of their medical issues.

It is also the case that attempting to provide equal care to all men in a society, while it is still a noble and admirable goal, might result in higher prices for the medical care at the same time that it causes shortages of goods and services. Supply and demand set the prices for the goods and services. If the demand for medical care is far greater than the supply, then the prices will increase for everyone, meaning that not only will the quality of the medical care decrease from the way that the system is overburdened, but the individual men who seek the medical care will have to pay more of their own money for a lower quality of care. Insofar as the prices increase, this will actually have the opposite effect. Rather than making medical care more widely available, or available for all of the men in the society, it will further restrict the access to medical care to only the men who have most material wealth and can afford to pay for it.

The same circumstances are also possible in other fields as well. If the field or profession itself does not have an adequate supply of goods or services for all of the men in the society, then trying to provide such things to all men equally will cause the prices to rise and any shortages to become even worse than they were already. The market operates according to particular rules, one of which is supply and demand. While market forces do not always operate in the best way for the production and distribution of material goods, it is still dangerous to ignore the ways that the market operates. Some men will unfortunately receive less of a share of the goods and services in society than other men. This is for the most part unavoidable. It is also not necessarily evil either, depending upon the particular case. Not all of the men in the society can or should have the exact same material wealth as everyone else. What the society ought to do, either by public or private means, is to make sure that all men have at least the ability to survive comfortably in life with the material goods that they earned from their own labor.

While men have a natural right to earn their material goods for their survival and delight by the work that they do for the society, it can never be said that anyone has a natural right to any material goods without having to work for them. It is contrary to justice for a man to receive a unearned good because other men worked to support him. The only possible case in which this is acceptable is when parents work to support their children. Yet even then, the parents support the children because the children will be able to benefit society later when they become adults. Hence the children allow the society to continue, which is part of the good for it. This is how the children are able to give back to the society for what they had received from it when their parent supported them. Whenever men cannot work to support themselves, and must depend upon the labor of others for their material goods, this is necessarily an act of almsgiving to the men who receive the support. And the men ought to recognize this and express gratitude for the way that the other men in the society are willing to support them when they cannot support themselves. It is good when men give material goods to support those who cannot support themselves, but this does not mean that the men supported have a right to those goods. And if a man refuses to work in the society when this is possible to him, he has violated one of the most essential rules of justice. He takes without giving back, meaning that he gets more than he deserves, which is inherently unjust.

When men come together in a society to work for the sake of their common good, it is inevitably the case that some men will work in positions in the society itself that are higher than others. Every society naturally needs one or more rulers, because it is necessary for there to be someone who can oversee what takes place in the whole society and thus determine what the men in the society need to do for the sake of their common good. Hence if there is some issue that the men in the society need to address more compared to some of the other problems, the ruler over the society can direct the men to deal with that issue before they handle some of the other issues. This way the society can benefit all the more from the order that is imposed and upheld by the ruler. This is the way that men form temporal states. The temporal state is the institution that is set over the society of men to work for the common material good of the men. The temporal state can take different forms based on how the men decide that they want to be ruled, but it is necessary that there always is a temporal state to rule over them. While men can do many things on their own for the sake of their own good, there must be some kind of order among them when they work together. Hence it is proper that there are some men appointed to oversee the order itself for the greater good of the whole society.

This is the way that human society itself is hierarchical. It was said that human society is supposed to be self-sufficient in a way that this cannot also be said for the individual men who together compose the society itself. So in the same way that the different parts of an animal body all work together for the animal itself to sustain life, the same can be said for the individual men who together compose the society. All of the men, both individually and severally, have some tasks that they can perform from which the whole society may benefit in some way. But there are some tasks that men can set out upon as members of the society that are higher or more essential for the good of the whole. Hence these men are higher in the social order than the other men. That some men are higher in the social order does not mean that the other men make contributions that the society itself can ever do without. All of the men can work in some way for the good of the whole. But since some men have a greater contribution by working in a higher or more essential function for the society, it is proper that the society itself recognizes this reality.

Now there are four ways that someone can be either higher or lower within the social order. First, this can happen because the role of the man in the society is more essential to the society than some other role. Hence the society could less do without this role being fulfilled than it can do without some other role being fulfilled. In this manner the ruler over the society is more essential to the whole, since the ruler provides the necessary direction for the rest of the society itself. Hence the whole society depends upon the ruler more than it does upon someone who does not exercise the same ultimate authority within the society. And since it would not be possible for one man to actually dictate in every single case what all of the men in the society ought to do, it is likewise necessary that there are lesser public authorities in the society itself to work for the greater good in more particular ways. Thus the ruler can have the advice of experts in different fields who can tell him how he should rule when it comes to one or another kind of issue, or the ruler can appoint subordinate rulers within the society who exercise a general authority over the different fields that exist, but only do so over certain local parts of the society itself. The authority can thus be either topical or regional. And in most cases it is necessary that different societies have both of these kinds of men to assist in the general rule over the society. The lesser rulers or advisors can have some share of the authority of the ruler over the whole society, so that they can act in his name and in accord with the authority that comes from him as the final authority in the society.

Second, it is possible that some men might be higher in the social order because even if they do not exercise a more essential role when compared to other men, they still do things for the good of the whole society that most of the men in the society itself are unable to do. This means that there will necessarily be a greater demand for their kind of work when compared to easier and more common pursuits. This means that these men are higher in the society as a result of the greater demand that comes for the things that they can provide to other men. Hence if a man works in a very difficult or learned profession, such as law or medicine, the man would be higher in the social order than someone who works in a less intense field that is more easily accessible to ordinary men according to their abilities. It is also likely that the men who work in such difficult fields or professions will receive more money for their work compared to other men who work in a field or profession that has less of a demand. The money that they receive for their work does not have to correspond to their place in the social order. Thus there can be some men who make more money while working in a lower field or profession that requires less skill, but for some reason also has a higher demand among the general population.

Third, it is possible that a man may be higher in the social order because the work that he does for the society as a whole pertains to higher faculties within men. This is similar to what was said about the difficulty of the field or profession in which the man works, but it is not strictly the same thing. So if a man is more concerned with intellectual work as opposed to bodily work, the intellectual would be higher in the social order because what he does involves a higher power in men in general. Bodily work can be difficult for men in its own way, and not all men have the ability to all of the different kinds of bodily work that are necessary for a society. But since the lower powers are more engaged when compared to the higher ones, the intellectual in this case would thus find himself in a higher social position than the man who does manual labor.

Fourth, the social order can be distinguished among men concerning the ends that exist for the different fields or professions in the society. Things exist for the sake of an end, meaning that the end makes the field or profession as the means thereto to be what it is. And the end is greater than the means because the means exists for the sake of the end. Hence a field or profession that pertains more to the end for men is greater than one that is more remote from it. Thus it is clear that a field or profession where the work done is for its own sake is better than one where the work is for the sake of some other good beyond it. This means that the more useful field or profession is actually lower than the less useful one, because to use something means that the thing itself is directed to an end beyond it rather than being sought as an end in itself. In this way it can be said that useless knowledge is greater than useful knowledge, because men seek the former directly for the sake of their delight while the latter is good primarily for the sake of something else. In this regard, it can be said that the contemplative life is higher than the active life, since the former is more for the end itself while the latter is the means to the end. More will be said about this when treating of the different states of life that exist in the Church on earth.

These are the different conditions that can be used to see if one's place in the social order is either higher or lower. The different fields or professions necessary to men in society vary also in terms of these qualities, meaning that some will be higher than the others. As it was mentioned, the money that men receive for their role in society does not necessarily correspond to their place in the social hierarchy. For example, a religious in the Church on earth is bound to live in poverty, meaning that he has very little if any material goods in his possession. Yet if the religious is a contemplative, he seeks God above all else, where God is the highest good that exists. So the contemplative religious would be in a higher social state than someone who is not a contemplative and who may have more material goods to his name. That someone has more material wealth does not have to mean that he is higher in the social order or that his role is more essential. The money that men receive for what they do in society is tied to the supply and demand for either the goods or services that they offer for the sake of other men, and these do not always have to correspond to whether the role fulfilled is higher or lower. Hence just because a man rules over the rest of the society, even if he is the sole ruler as in the case of a monarchy, does not have to mean that he has the most material wealth at his disposal. Someone else might earn more money as a private subject within the society, so that the ruler of the society has less money or material goods. While supply and demand can be used in some ways to determine a just remuneration for men for what they contribute to the society, it is not a perfect system. This was already evident from what was said concerning economics and the regulations of the market that are necessary to keep the market as just as possible for the good of the society.

Hence there are different ways to determine if someone occupies either a higher or lower place in the social order. It is also the case that men who work in the same field or profession may be either higher or lower within that profession as well. So while one field or profession may necessarily be higher or lower than another field or profession, the lower men in the given field or profession might overlap in some way with a lower profession. And the men who are higher in the same field or profession might be lower than men in the next highest field or profession. In this way it is evident that the different places within the roles of society are vertical arrangements rather than horizontal ones. Just because a man is in a field or profession that may be considered lower than another does not have to mean that he is necessarily below the next highest field or profession given the ways that they all overlap with each other.

It is also necessary to address the role of the poor in society. There will always be the poor in any human society, if for no other reason than that some men can earn more money for themselves using their abilities when compared to other men. It can also be said that since money is needed for men to make more money, some men might be poor not because of a lack of ability or effort, but simply because they did not have the same opportunities as the other men in the society. Thus a man with less ability or perhaps making less of an effort might rise higher in the social order to earn more money than someone who has less opportunity. The man who has the greater opportunity can spend money to get the education or training that he needs to rise higher within the society, while the other man may not rise as high simply because he lacked the money to put his abilities to good use. He did not make the same effort because no one ever gave him the possibility to make the effort to rise higher. This is one of the ways that poverty can be consistent among men across many generations. The poor have children who also remain poor because they lacked the ability to make a better life for themselves. Hence it is inevitable that there will always be the poor in any society, however unfortunate it may be that some men are deprived in this manner.

Since the poor in society are often poor because of things beyond their control, such as the lack of opportunity to rise out of their poverty, the men in the society who have more money should do what they can where possible to help the poor. This means that they can be merciful to them and offer them either some money or even material goods that they are lacking so that they are not as deprived. And if the wealthier men in the society have a way to help the poor rise out of their poverty, then they can give them the help to find work so that they can better support themselves. It is never proper for the wealthier men in the society to look down upon those who do not have as much as they do, considering that many of the poor are such not because they lack ability or effort, but because they never had the possibility to earn more money for themselves or for their families. Hence the wealthier men in the society must always remember that having more money or being higher in the social order does not make them more virtuous men.

The virtue of individual men is the primary way that some men might be considered better than other men. Being higher in the social order does not have to mean that a man is more virtuous. Much less is it the case that greater material wealth, which is not distributed to men in society according to either virtue or their place in the social order, that makes men either better or worse. If anything it can be said that wealthier men have greater difficulty living in proper virtue because of their material wealth. The men who have greater material wealth will have to set apart more time and effort to manage all of their material wealth, meaning that they will take away time from higher pursuits, such as the spiritual goods that are also possible to men in life. And if the men receive more delight from their greater material wealth, they will have less of a desire for the higher spiritual goods that are possible to them at the same time, meaning that they will neglect the higher for the sake of the lower. So it would be entirely wrong to assume that a man who has more money or more material goods in life would necessarily be better than someone who lacks these things. There is almost an inverse correlation that exists, although this is not entirely the case either. So men of greater wealth are not better than other men because of their wealth, and the men who are higher in the social order are also not necessarily greater than those below them.

There is also the quality of the work that the men can do in their field or profession for the good of the whole society. This is separate from the man's place within the social order. Hence two men can be in the same place in the social order, working within the same field. But one man will do what he does much better than the other. It is possible that the man who does his work with a better quality will rise higher within his field or profession. This can be a reward to him for the way that he produced better work than the other men. But it is not always the case that the men who do best what they do in their field or profession necessarily rise to the higher states within the field or profession itself. As it was said, the opportunities that some men have are greater than other men. This can affect the kind of work that they do, so that the man who does better work had more of an education or training for him to do the work better. Thus he will rise higher when men see that he does better work. Yet at the same time, the man who does work of a lesser quality might even have more of an ability to do the work, but does not do the better work because he lacked the opportunity to learn more how to better perform his tasks. Hence it is evident that ability, quality, and opportunity all operate independent of each other, and all of them affect a man's place within the social order in its own way.

There is always the possibility of corruption as well. The man who does the better work might deserve to rise higher in his field or profession, but because the man whose work is of a lesser quality has some social connections, the latter will rise higher than the former. It may even be that if a man produces a better quality of work compared to the other men, the men who decide to promote men will keep him in the same place because of the good work that he does there. They will not want to lose his better quality work by promoting him to a higher place where he might supervise the work of other men, but then not actually do the work himself. He might deserve the promotion because of his strong performance in his field or profession, but someone else will get it precisely because the other men involved do not want to lose the benefits derived from keeping him where he is at the time.

Then there is the possibility that while a man works in one or another field or profession, and he is very good at working in his current position, this does not have to mean that he would be good or better in a higher one. If a man does something good for the rest of the society through his work, this does not mean that he should be promoted to a higher position where he would have to supervise the work of the other men. Just because the man is good at where he works does not mean that he necessarily has the supervisory or administrative abilities to lead the other men.

The man might also not have the personal skills to be set over the other men either, where dealing with the other men will be an essential part of the higher position itself. On the other hand, there may be a man who is in the same lower position and whose quality of work is not as good, but who does have better supervisory or administrative skills, meaning that he can better serve the society if he is promoted over the other man. The individual men should also consider if they possess the intellectual or personal skills to take on higher positions in their field or profession. They may think that they deserve to be promoted to a leadership position because they do good work, but they would not be good in the leadership position after all because it requires different skills than the ones that they use where they are. This does not mean that their current contribution is less valuable to the society. It simply means that they would not be able to manage doing a different kind of work, even if it is in the same field or profession.

These are all the different things that affect a man's place within the social order. So while there is the distinction of higher and lower among men in society, the ways that can determine if a man himself is higher or lower are many and varied. And just because a man in the society is not as high as some other man does not mean that he is less valuable for that reason. This is evident according to what has been said.

Thus far the different roles in human society that have been considered are all the roles that are held by free men. But it is also possible that a society might tolerate slavery among men. By definition, a slave is a man whose body is owned by another man. Since men are composed of soul and body, and ownership is an act of the will that derives from the soul, it is indeed possible for one man to own the body of another man. And since the institution of slavery has existed in many different societies throughout human history, it is necessary to consider the role that slavery plays in human society when addressing the social order. Slaves are clearly the lowest men within the social order, but they are part of the social order all the same.

Since it is indeed possible for one man to own another man, and there is clearly hierarchy that exists in human society, it stands to reason that there is nothing unnatural about slavery in itself. Men naturally possess free will, which they use for the sake of some greater good. But it is also evident that different men within human society have different degrees of their own freedom. Some men can exercise their free will to a greater degree than other men. Children gradually come into the use of their free will as they grow older, yet they still have less freedom for a time after they have begun to use their free will. They need time to learn and mature so that they can more effectively use their free will for the sake of a greater good. And it is also the case that a man who works for other men has less use over his free will than the men for whom he works. The entire society as a whole has less freedom than the ultimate ruler over the society, since the men in the society have bound themselves in some way to obey his rule for the sake of their own good. So if freedom exists in degrees among men within a society, which is evident from what has just been said, then it stands to reason that there will be men in society that will have the least freedom of all. These men are the slaves, who work for the sake of the other men who own their bodies and thus have the ability to use them for the sake of their work. The lack of freedom in the slave does not, for this reason, contradict the way that God gave free will to all men as such.

But while it is possible for men to be slaves, this does not mean that slavery is a beneficial or desirable state for a society. It was said that men will do better work if they work for the sake of their own immediate good. Having a stake in the goods that their own labor produces means that they will produce a higher quality of goods and services for the society itself, with the effect that the society as a whole will benefit more. And it is the nature of a slave that he works for the good of other men rather than for his own good. His master must necessarily support him in order for him to continue to do his work while enslaved. Since there is an lack of essential connection from what the slave does when he works and what he gets in return in order for him to work, this is a less efficient system than a society that supports itself by free labor. The slave has less reason to be concerned with the quality of his work because there is no natural connection between the work that he does and what he receives for his survival. So while slavery is indeed possible within human society, it is not at all a desirable state either for individual men or for the good of the whole ociety.

There are also many abuses that can take place concerning slavery. It was said that the institution of slavery itself is not immoral or contrary to nature. But in order for slavery to exist in a moral context, the basic humanity of the slave must be recognized. Hence he cannot be treated as less than a man endowed with a body and a soul. He has a rational intellect and free will in the same manner as other men. To treat a man as less than a man, even in the event that he is enslaved, would be a grave sin against the nature of the man himself. This would be to disparage what

God had made, since God made him to be a man. And it would be contrary to justice, since justice is to give to all things what they deserve as what they are. Hence the other men must treat the slave with the proper respect due to him as a man. He cannot be treated as an animal or as an inanimate object, which would be to give him less than the respect that he deserves as a man.

Similarly the basic human needs and desires of men should also be recognized in the slave despite his state in the society. Hence the master has an obligation to provide him with things like food, clothing, and shelter. And while the master owns the work that the slave does for him, the master cannot overwork the slave either, since this would be contrary to his good as a man. Men need time to rest so that they can continue to live and serve society as a whole.

Since men as such are endowed with a soul from which they exercise the powers of the rational intellect and free will, it is possible for men to know about God as well. This means that all men as such have spiritual obligations to God in addition to what they do in the created world. This applies no less to a slave than it does to other men. Thus in order for the master to recognize the basic humanity of the slave, he should give off time for the slave to properly love God and fulfill the religious obligations that he owes to God above all else.

These are the different ways that men can own slaves in accord with proper virtue. But it was still said all the same that slavery is not a desirable or beneficial state for men in any society, meaning that it is best if slavery does not exist, except perhaps as a punishment for criminals who have been justly convicted of crimes against the whole society. The loss of freedom when the criminal is reduced to a state of servitude can be a proper way for him to pay back to his society for what he took from it by the crime he committed. Since the criminal is held in bondage, this can also keep him from committing more crimes in the future, which he might do if he was allowed to go free. This is the only condition in which it might be preferable for men to live in this state.

While it is possible for men to be enslaved, and it is also not inherently contrary to proper virtue for men to own slaves, a system of slavery based on race is always contrary to proper virtue and to natural law. While there are different kinds of men that live in the world, men with different appearances or who have different cultures, it cannot be said that any one group of men on account of these things should be reduced to slavery. This would be to ignore the necessary differences that exist among men on an individual level, and it would also be an arbitrary distinction among men at the same time. That one man may come from a different culture or perhaps look different from other men does not have to mean that he is necessarily less than the other men for those reasons. Much less is it inevitable that all of the men like him are necessarily inferior to the men of other cultures or who have different appearances. Some men may be superior or inferior to other men in many different ways, particularly in terms of virtue. But there is nothing to say that all of the men who share those qualities have to be inferior to different kinds of men. This would ignore the role of free will that exists among all men as such. Men of different cultures might be better or worse at certain tasks based on the particular customs or habits that their cultures have developed over time. But given the variations that exist both among the different cultures and among individual men, it would be next to impossible to compare the different cultures of men to determine which one is better or worse than the others. And even if one culture may be better than other cultures, not all of the men in the culture necessarily have to conform to its customs or habits. Hence to base the institution of slavery on categories such as race is arbitrary and contrary to the natural law. Since this would mean that some men would necessarily receive less of the good for conditions that are beyond their control, this would be a very grave injustice.

It must also be considered the different relations that can form among men when one or more of the men is enslaved. The master owns the slave's body, which is the essential nature of slavery itself. And the master can use the slave's body for purposes of work. Yet at the same time, this does not mean that a master can use the slave for any other purpose, as the purpose of the ownership in the first place is only for the sake of work. Hence if a master was to use a female slave for the purposes of sex, this would be gravely immoral, not only because sex is only supposed to be within the context of marriage, but also because the master does not own the slave for that purpose as well. This would be the case even if the female slave was to consent to the sexual act with the master. The same rules that apply in terms of the moral concerns of human interaction would mostly apply here in the same way as well. This means that a slave would also be allowed to have some legal recourse against a master who acted contrary to his natural rights.

It may be that a slave also seeks to get married while he is in this state. Now since the master owns the slave's body, and the slave must use his body in marriage for purposes of sex with his wife, the master must give his consent for the slave to get married. Yet with the consent of the master, the marriage contract formed between the man and woman if one of them is enslaved is still legitimate. And in the event that the marriage of the man and woman with one or both of them being enslaved was to produce children, the children would have to be free even though they were descended from slaves. It would be unjust for the children to remain in this state simply because their parents were enslaved. The parents could still raise the children as they saw proper, because this is a natural right that no human institution can compromise, which would necessarily include slavery. And given that the family has natural rights of its own which the society itself must respect, even a society that tolerates the institution of slavery must work to preserve the families of the enslaved. It would be morally unjust for the enslaved parents to be separated from their children, as their natural right to remain together as a family overrides any right of the master to sell the slave so that the slave would be separated from his family.

Once a man is enslaved, it is also proper that some prospect of freedom is given to him unless his servitude is due to a crime that he had committed. In the case that he is a criminal, he might have shown by the nature of the crime committed that he does not deserve to live freely in society, meaning that his enslavement can remain for the rest of his natural life. But if someone is enslaved for some other reason, then it is proper that there is a way for him to leave his state and become free, much as the society ought to allow men in other lower states to rise above those states by their own power. Hence it makes sense that the society would allow slaves to buy their freedom, or for other men who are already free to purchase them for the purpose of freeing them. As it was said, while slavery is not essentially a moral issue, it is best that a society does not have slavery at all, since the society as a whole can function better in the event that men are able to freely work for the sake of their own good rather than having to work for other men while being owned by those other men.

So it is clear that there is no inherent moral problem with slavery, but at the same time this does not mean that it is acceptable as the basis for the economy of a society, since it is better for men can be able to work freely for the sake of the goods that they need in order for them to survive and have a reasonable degree of delight in life. Slavery can also lend itself to different kinds of corruption which mean that the essential humanity of the slave and his natural rights have been disregarded. It is true that basically anything in the fallen world can be subject to corruption, and that such corruption does not inherently rule out the use of the thing itself. This is the case with slavery as it would be with anything else. Hence if slavery in any form is tolerated in a society, aside for being a form of punishment for criminals, it can still be done with proper virtue, although it is best avoided because it does not coincide with a proper economic system for men.

Wherefore the extent of the natural law has been considered based on what was said. The natural law is a kind of law that inheres in the nature of things as what they are. Since the different things that exist in the created world can all obtain some good in accord with their nature as what they are, an examination of the nature of different things can show how the thing itself ought to act for the sake of its own benefit. And when the object acts in accord with its own good, this is according to the principles of justice. Justice also concerns rights, which can be classified as being either natural rights or positive rights. While all rights as such are circumstantial, the natural rights of men concern unchangeable circumstances. So while they do not inhere in human nature as such, they still must always be upheld because the circumstances are grounded in human nature, which is the same for all men throughout all time and place. Positive rights can differ from one place to another, since the positive right is based on circumstances that do change from time and place. The different rights that fall under one or the other category have been considered, as well as the ways that human free will plays a role in the ways that the society itself works to uphold these rights. While men are all possessed of a rational intellect and free will, there is still naturally a social hierarchy among them, which has also been considered.

Thus far the end of law has been considered mostly in terms of the proximate goods for the subject. This is because the natural law as such pertains to goods that exist in nature, which means that they are present in the created world. Yet since God gave men a rational intellect and free will, men can come to know and love God in life in the hope of union with God in the afterlife. And since God made men for Himself, God works in the created world to bring men to Him. God does this by means of the Old Law and the New Law, which are the two different parts of the Divine law. It is the Divine law that must now be considered one of the four forms of law.

CHAPTER III.
THE OLD LAW

The Divine law is distinct from the eternal law even though the names would appear to make them the same thing. The eternal law was said to be the sovereign type that exists in the Divine essence Itself, while the Divine law is the will of God manifested to fallen men for the sake of a particular purpose. The understanding of the Divine law in general is inseparable from the end for Which God intended it, since things exist for the sake of an end. The Divine law is the means to an end, and the end is God Himself.

It was explained that God alone is essentially good because being is the same thing as goodness and the Divine essence is existence Itself. This means that all that God does must always be good, because the effect must be in the cause in order for it to be the effect of that cause, and there is nothing in God that is not the essential goodness of the Divine essence Itself. This is consistent with how the Divine essence alone is perfectly simple, meaning that God alone is not composed of parts. The Divine essence is existence Itself, and being is goodness, meaning that God is His own essential goodness and nothing else. All other things that exist are good only insofar as they participate in the essential goodness of the Divine essence Itself. Since God alone is essentially good in this manner, all that God does in all cases must always be good.

And since things are defined by their ends, as the end makes the means to be what it is, this means that the end for which God works is always the greatest possible good in every case. Since being is the same thing as goodness, God is good to all things when He wills that they exist through His own essence. This is how God created the entire world and how He sustains it in being once He created it. That God made all things from nothing and that God allows all things to be what they are once He made them are both expressions of the way that God wills the greatest possible good for all things.

As God wills all that He wills in every case for the sake of the greatest possible good, it can be said that God wills all things ultimately for the sake of His own essence, as the Divine essence alone is essentially good. This is how God is both the beginning and the end of all other things that exist. So if God is both the beginning and the end of all other things that exist, not only is God good to all things by making them and sustaining them in being as what they are, but He is also good to them by bringing them back to His essence in the end. The fulfillment of all that God has made is in the Divine essence Itself from Which God made all things in the first place. And it was said that God had made the entire created world from nothing.

Now when God wills the greatest possible good for all things that exist, this is the very definition of love. Love in general is for the subject to desire the greatest possible good for the object. Hence when God wills that all things exist and that they all reach their ultimate end in the essential goodness of His own essence, these are the ways that God loves all things. It can even be said that God Himself is love. Love is the desire for the greatest possible good, and God makes all things good by His essence in these ways. Since God is pure act without any potentiality, it does not suffice to say that God simply desires the good for the object, since desire is potentiality, and there is no potentiality in God. So God loves all things when He actually gives them the good in these different ways. Hence God is love, and God's love is the ultimate power that moves the entire created world. An understanding of the movement of different objects within the created world cannot be separated from the knowledge of God's love as the power that moves it. God made the created world and fulfills it in His essence because of His love for all things.

Thus the fulfillment of the entire created world in the Divine essence is the work of God's love for all things. Hence all created natures came out of God when God made them and they are all reconciled back to God each in their own way. God also made all different created natures so that He can share His own essential goodness with them each in His own way. This is the reason that God made all things. God perfectly delights in His own essence, since His essence contains the essences of all other things that exist. But God willed to share His own essential goodness with other things by the way that He made them all from nothing. This is why God chose to create the world. God's creation of the world was thus an expression of His love, because to give the good to all things by their very being is consistent with the definition of love.

And God made the angels and men in particular with a rational intellect and free will. It was said that there is a natural hierarchy of things that exist in the created world. This hierarchy is arranged so that what is higher is more like God and can come closer to God than what is lower. Since God gave to the angels and men a rational intellect and free will, they can use these powers to know and love God. Then they can come to be with God in the state of beatitude. This is how the angels and men as rational beings can obtain to their ultimate end in the Divine essence Itself. The state of beatitude is when the rational subject is united to the Divine essence, and so sees God as God is. Since the rational subject is united to God in the state of beatitude in this manner, he is perfected in all of his faculties by the union with the Divine essence. This is the way that the rational subject with God in the state of beatitude has the most perfect delight from God in that state, where delight is defined as the experience of the good once it has been obtained.

    Now the angels all reached their ultimate end by one act after God made them. Men receive all of their information about the created world from the external senses of the body, meaning that men receive more information over time into the rational intellect through the external senses. The same is not the case for the angels because they lack bodies and external senses. So the angel receives all of his knowledge about the created world from his own essence. Since the angels are the highest being in God's creation, being below only God Himself, this means that the essences of all lower created natures are contained in the angelic essence much as they are contained in the Divine essence. The only difference is that they are more perfectly in God than in the angels. This is because the lower is also naturally present in the higher. So when the angel turns to understand his own essence, he receives all of his knowledge about the created world at once through the essence itself. Thus the angel's knowledge of things is not discursive. The angel knows all that he can know at once without being able to add any new knowledge of what he did not already know. The angel can still come into a greater knowledge of things that he already knew in some sense, but he cannot come into knowledge of something entirely new that he never knew at all. Since it takes new information for the subject to change back and forth from either good or evil to the converse, and the angel knows all that he knows at once, the angels were confirmed in the state of either good or evil after God had initially made them. Thus the good angels came into the state of beatitude with God while the evil angels were condemned to hell for the way that they had rejected God. In this way it is not possible for the evil angels to ever be saved. They became the demons and they remain as such forever after.

    The case is different for men. God made men so that they can receive new information from the external senses of the body, and the external senses deliver their new information to the rational intellect that derives from the soul. So if men can receive new information, they can go back and forth from either good or evil to the converse. This means that evil men can become good while good men can become evil. This is how it is possible for men in life to possibly be saved in a way that salvation is not also possible to the fallen angels. The fallen angels cannot be saved, but fallen men can still repent while they are alive so that they can come to be with God in the state of beatitude in the end. This is why God chose to save fallen men, while God did not do the same for the fallen angels. The nature of the angelic knowledge itself precludes the possibility that an angel can repent of the sins that he had previously committed in order to come to God in the end.

While one third of the angels fell from the original grace and virtue in which God had made them and thus became the demons, all ordinary men suffered from their Fall. The devil, who had been the highest of all of the angels and thus the highest individual created nature that God had made, became proud because he was above the rest of God's creation. This is how the devil was moved to disobey God. The devil thought that he was better than he really is, which is the definition of pride. Pride was the first sin and the most important sin that the devil committed. This is how he was confirmed in his evil after God made him. Then he chose to tempt the first men so that they also disobeyed God and lost the original grace and virtue in which God had made them. This is how sin and imperfection entered into the created world. God had made all things perfectly, since all that God does is perfect because His essence is perfect, and the effect always resembles the cause in order for it to be the effect of that cause. Hence God did not make anything in an imperfect state. The imperfection only entered into the created world because the devil fell from the original grace and virtue of his own accord and then tempted the first men to do the same because of how he tempted them.

When the first men fell from the original grace and virtue in which God had made them, they committed the original sin. Now since people come into the world from other people, the guilt for the original sin was passed from parent to child along with the defects of the fallen human nature. The soul is naturally united to the body, even though God makes the souls of men directly while the body is conceived in the sexual act. The soul thus created is united to the body as the form thereof with the body itself as the matter. Since the soul and body are naturally united, the guilt and the imperfection from the original sin passed from the body to the soul through the natural union of these two parts. This is how men came to be fallen. At the same time that men received their fallen nature in this way because of the original sin, the rest of the created world also suffered from disorders as the result of what the first men had done. The higher naturally orders the lower, which means that when the disorder of sin and imperfection had entered into men as the higher power, the rest of the lower world also suffered from the disorder at the same time. This is how the rest of the natural world does not obey the commands of men as the higher power, which had been the case when men lived in the state of the original grace and virtue. Men had perfect dominion over the rest of the material world because they are both spiritual and material beings, and the spiritual is higher than the material because it is more like God Who is pure spirit. This was the way that men had the natural ability in the state of the original grace and virtue to command the lower created natures that exist. But since the first men disobeyed God, God chose to punish them so that the lower created natures would disobey them in turn.

Now it might seem that God allowing the sin and imperfection to disrupt the created world that He had so perfectly made would be contrary to the way that God wills the greatest possible good for all things in every case. The disorder in the created world means that there is a lack of the possible good. And God still works to sustain all things in being as what they are despite the ways that they suffer from these disorders. But it is also the case that God allows evil to exist in order to bring some good even out of evil. Thus God allowed the evil to enter into the created world in these ways for the sake of some good. Fallen men could better understand the good from the contrast with the evil they experience. This means that they can choose the good over the evil and thus act in accord with proper virtue. Acting in accord with proper virtue makes them better, so that they become the proximate cause of the good that they do, with God Himself as the ultimate cause thereof. As the cause of a thing being such is yet more so, the men become better in this way. This means that God out of His perfect justice can give men a greater good for the good that they were able to do by their free will. This is how God allowed the evil to enter into the created world. God uses the evil to get men to merit a much greater good from Him than they could have ever received if they had remained in the state of the original grace and virtue in which God had made them. The greater good is to come to be united to God Himself in the state of beatitude, where they can experience the most perfect delight possible to them as rational beings.

    This is the way that God seeks to reconcile the entire created world in general and fallen mankind in particular with His essence. Since God knows all things that can possibly be known through His essence, God knew perfectly from the very beginning that the angels and men would bring about the Fall from the misuse of the free will that He gave them. God allowed for this to happen so that He could perfect the created world by His essence, giving all things a greater good than the good that they had received from Him in the first place. This is how God works to bring all things back to Himself in the end. God works to accomplish this for fallen men in particular by the Divine law.

It was said that God allowed men to fall from the state of the original grace and virtue in which He had made them so that they could learn to experience the difference between good and evil. When the first men committed the original sin, they chose the evil over the good. This is the nature of sin as such. It was said that being is the same thing as goodness because the good is desirable, and all things desire being above all else, since it is from being that they come into other good things. As being is the same thing as goodness and evil is opposed to the good, evil is the lack of the being that can be present but is not present in the given case. And when men act for the sake of a lesser good over the greatest possible good, they choose the evil over the good. This does not mean that the lesser good as such is not good, but that it lacks some of the being that is present in the greatest possible good in that case.

Hence the man who acts for the sake of a lesser good chooses the object that lacks some possible being. The effect of this choice is that he moves further away from God. God alone is essentially good because being is the same thing as goodness and the Divine essence is existence Itself. And what is essentially so is more so than what is only by participation. This means that God alone is greater than all other things that exist. So when the men choose the greatest possible good in the given case over any lesser possible goods, they choose what is more like God over what is less like God. Hence they can use this choice to come closer to God over time so that they can possibly be saved when they die. This is how they can come to be with God in the state of beatitude, where they can experience the greatest delight possible to them as who they are, where delight is the experience of the good once it has been obtained. But when men choose a lesser possible good over the greatest possible good, they choose what is less like God over what is more like God, meaning that they move further away from God because they rejected God. If they die in their sin, they will be sent to hell to suffer forever for the ways that they had rejected God in life.

This is the nature of both virtue and sin, and it is the way that men need to live in proper virtue if they are to come to God. But it is also the case that men would not be able to come to God in the state of beatitude on their own even if they were to live in proper virtue. They still need the help that God alone chooses to provide to men for this purpose. Nothing can rise above itself by its own power. It can only come to things at its own level or beneath it. This means that men still need help from God in order to come to God in the state of beatitude, as God alone is above all of His creation because He alone is the first cause of all other things that exist, and the cause of a thing being such is yet more so. Thus while men can live in proper virtue according to their own natural abilities, this in itself is not sufficient to bring the men to God in the state of beatitude.

Since men as such lack the ability to rise above their level by their own power in order to come to God in beatitude, it is necessary for men to use the help that God gives to men for that end. Now God did not have to choose to save men at all, regardless of whether men had fallen into sin. God could have allowed men to either remain in the state of the original grace and virtue in the event that men had not sinned or He could have allowed all fallen men as such to go to hell when they die for the way that they had sinned against Him, both by the original sin and by the different personal sins that men have committed against Him. But God out of His own abundant mercy chose to save men, making it possible for them to come to be with God in the state of beatitude. Mercy was said to be to spare a thing from the evil that it deserves as what it is. God is merciful to all things when He sustains them all in being as what they are by His essence Which is existence Itself. Thus God gives all things their being as what they are, meaning that He also spares them from the contrary evil of non-being into which they would fall if God did not choose to sustain them in being in the way that He does. So God is merciful to all things in this manner.

    God chose out of His abundant mercy to save fallen men despite the ways that they had sinned against Him. Men did nothing of their own accord to warrant God choosing to save them. Men could never merit enough for God to choose to bring them into the state of beatitude even if they had not sinned at all. To be with God in the state of beatitude is for the subject to experience the infinite goodness of the Divine essence. And it is impossible for the finite created subject to ever merit an infinite good. The infinite is greater than the finite, meaning that the finite created subject can never be the cause of an infinite good. This would make the infinite to be contained within the finite, as the effect must always be present in the cause in order for it to be the effect of that cause. And the greater cannot be contained in the lesser because that would make the lesser to be greater, which is contradictory. So it is impossible for any created subject to ever merit an infinite good. Since the rational subject receives an infinite good from God when he comes to be with God in the state of beatitude, it is altogether impossible for the rational subject to come to God by his own merit. In this way and for this reason, men did nothing of their own accord for God to will to save them. God chose to save men simply for the sake of His own reasons. Men merit from God when they do the good in response to the help that He gives them, but they cannot merit in the first place for God to save them. This is beyond the abilities of men as finite beings. This is clear from what has been said.

Yet while men did nothing of their own accord in order for God to choose to save them, it is still the case that men need to respond to God working to save them by their own free will. God gave men their free will in the first place so that they can choose the good over the evil, meaning that they can become the proximate cause of the good that they do in this way, with God Himself as the ultimate cause thereof. From the way that men do the good, God can give them some good in return in accord with His perfect justice. This is the way that God chooses to bring men to be with Him in the state of beatitude. God moves some men externally by the Divine grace and virtue so that they can accept the same internally and thus be saved when they die. God is merciful to men in the first place when He moves the men externally by the Divine grace and virtue, and He is just when He gives the good to the men who choose by their free will to internally accept the Divine grace and virtue. Thus it can be said that God saving men in this way is an act of the Divine justice within the context of the Divine mercy. This is the way that men can come to be with God in beatitude when they die.

But in order for men to internally accept the Divine grace and virtue once God has moved them to act in this way, God must make the Divine grace and virtue available to men in some way for them to accept it. This was the work of the Divine law. For God to offer the Divine grace and virtue to fallen men for them to eventually be saved, God chose to gradually bring men back to Him over time. Thus the Divine law itself is divided into the Old Law and the New Law. The Old Law is what God had revealed of Himself to the Jews in order to prepare fallen men in general to receive Christ in the New Law. And it is from Christ in the New Law that men can receive the actual Divine grace and virtue by which they can be saved. The Old Law was thus the preparation for men to receive the Divine grace and virtue from Christ under the New Law. To prepare men to receive the Divine grace and virtue from Christ under the New Law, much of what took place in the time of the Old Law prefigured the events of the New Law. Thus the Jews in the time of the Old Law knew and loved Christ in figure but they could not do this in reality because Christ had not yet come to earth, as He would eventually at the time of the First Coming. Yet because the Jews were able to adore Christ in figure in the time of the Old Law, they received the figure of the Divine grace and virtue as opposed to the reality thereof. Since the Old Law was the preparation for the New Law, it would not have made sense for God to give the reality of the Divine grace and virtue to the Jews while they were still being prepared to receive the same. This would not make any sense. So the Jews in the time of the Old Law had received from God the figure of the Divine grace and virtue in place of the reality. All of the actual Divine grace and virtue that comes to men for the men to be saved comes from Christ on the Cross, which means that men have to choose to unite themselves to Christ on the Cross if they are to be saved when they die.

Wherefore it is evident from what has been said that no man can ever come to God in the state of beatitude without the help that God alone can provide. And it is the case that God made human nature in order for men to come to be with Him in beatitude. This was the way that God gave men a rational intellect and free will. The rational intellect of men can understand universal things, which means that men can come to know God Who is the most universal of things because He alone is the first cause of all other things that exist, and the cause of a thing being such is yet more so. Thus men have the natural ability to use their rational intellect to know God. Once they know God by their rational intellect, they can come to desire God by the free will that derives from it. The will that derives from the rational intellect is necessarily a free will. The rational intellect can make complex distinctions, which means that the men can choose among the different things that were distinguished using the will that derives from it. Since the will has more choices, it is necessarily a free will, where choice is the essence of freedom. So God gave men a rational intellect and free will so that they can know Him and love Him, and can come to be with Him in the state of beatitude when they die. Since God alone is the highest good to Whom men can attain, men ought to make God the ultimate end of all that they do in life. They should do all that they do so that what they do can bring them closer to God in the end.

Now while God chose to reveal Himself to men as part of the way for men to be saved, men can still know certain things about God even without the Divine revelation. It is evident that men throughout history have been able to know that God exists and even to properly understand some of the Divine attributes as well. In this way Aristotle was able to demonstrate the existence of God using natural reason, and to conclude at the same time that God's essence is existence Itself. There are other Divine attributes that men can know using only their natural reason. It is not strictly necessary for God to reveal these things in order for men to properly know about them. Men can learn these things about God even without the Divine revelation.

But God still chose to reveal Himself to men after a time for the ultimate purpose of saving them. While men can use their natural reason to know that God exists and to know certain attributes of the Divine essence Itself, if men had to solely rely on their natural reason in order for them to know God, it might be possible for the men to be in error about what they think that they know. As God alone is essentially good, God alone is supremely reliable. Hence God alone can neither deceive nor be deceived. So when men rely on their own natural abilities to know God, there is always the possibility that they might be in error. Yet because God can never be in error, when men rely on God to know things, they can be sure that what God has revealed to them must be true. The men themselves might be mistaken about the nature of what God revealed or whether it was even God Who revealed some things to them. But if they correctly identify something as coming from God, and they can rule out the possibility that they misinterpreted certain things, they can know with certainty the truth of what God had revealed to them. This means that God is trustworthy above all else, since God knows all things and God can neither deceive nor be deceived in any way.

It is also the case that God choosing to reveal Himself to men was so that men could know that it is possible for them to come to be with God in the state of beatitude. While men in the fallen state can still use their natural reason in order for them to know God, this does not mean that they can know that there is a way to come to God in the state of beatitude, or what the way to God really is in the event that it exists at all. And since men cannot come to God all on their own, God must show men the way to come to Him. This is the way that God chose to save fallen men so that they can come to be with Him in the state of beatitude when they die.

Now God first began the Divine revelation under the Old Law in the time of Abraham, who was the father of the entire Jewish people. God had entrusted the revelation of Himself initially only to Abraham and his family. God had continued to lead them for several generations until He sent them into Egypt in order to escape from the famine that was taking place within the promised land at the time. It was when the Jews were in Egypt that they became a great nation. Since the Jews had increased in number in Egypt as they became a nation, they were eventually reduced to slavery by the Egyptians. Their slavery lasted until Moses led them back to the promised land and to their freedom. It was when God had led the Jews through Moses back to the promised land that He revealed to them the essential precepts of the Old Law. The observance of the Old Law gave the Jews an understanding through the precepts thereof about what it would take for men in general to merit from God once Christ at the time of the First Coming had established the New Law for men to be saved.

The Old Law in itself contained many different precepts that it was incumbent upon the Jews to observe. And when the Jews had failed to properly observe the different precepts that God had given to them, they were duly punished for their disobedience. This is how God had sought to instruct fallen mankind in general through the works of the Jews for fallen men to learn the difference between right and wrong, between good and evil. Fallen men could learn from the example of the Jews how they could come into more of the good when they acted with proper virtue, and how they would lose more of the good if they were to sin. This is the case not only as the inevitable result of their virtue or sin, but also because of the ways that God would either directly reward or punish them for the different things that they had done by their free will.

It was necessary for God in this way to instruct the Jews in the differences between right and wrong and the importance of living in proper virtue. Sin darkens the powers of the rational intellect of men. To sin is choose a lesser good over the greatest possible good in the given case. This means that the men follow their passions instead of what they know in the rational intellect. Now the passions of men know only the particulars without also being aware of the universals. This is the nature of the passions as such, and it is not a consequence of the Fall. God gave men their passions in order to move them more easily to the greatest possible good that they understood in the rational intellect. Hence it is proper that the rational intellect should identify the good to be desired, and that the passions would assist the man to move in his free will for the sake of the greatest possible good. This way the man can attain to the delight that is possible to him from the possession of the greatest possible good. And it was the case in the state of the original grace and virtue that men could command their passions using the rational intellect and free will. The rational intellect is above the passions because the rational intellect is aware of the universals while the passions know only the particulars. Now the universal is greater than the particular, and the end makes the means to be what it is. As the end for the rational intellect is greater than the end for the passions, it can be said that the rational intellect is higher than the passions. And the higher naturally orders the lower. Since God made men properly when He established them in the state of the original grace and virtue, God made it so that the men in their original state could use their rational intellect and the free will that derives from it to command their passions for the sake of obtaining the greatest possible good in the given case.

But when men fell from the state of the original grace and virtue in which God had made them, the passions were able to defy the orders of the rational intellect and free will. This disobedience of these powers is possible because the passions are only aware of the particulars without also being aware of the universals. So when men fell from the original grace and virtue, the rational intellect and free will lost their ability to command the passions. This was one of the consequences of the Fall. Just as the first men had disobeyed God Who is above them, God punished men so that the passions of men disobey the rational intellect and free will which are above them. So when men choose to follow their passions without regard for what they know in the rational intellect, they can act for the sake of a lesser good instead of the greatest possible good in the given case. They ignore that they act for the sake of a lesser good when they follow their passions in this manner. And when men choose to obey their passions instead of what they know in the rational intellect, this causes the passions to grow stronger from how they repeatedly gratify them by the lesser goods that they seek to obtain. As the passions grow stronger, they prevent the men from being able to objectively find the greatest possible good for them in the given case. This is how sin darkens the intellect. Now since God had allowed mankind to fall into serious degrees of sin between the time of the original sin and the beginning of the Old Law, it was thus necessary for God to teach men through the Jews under the Old Law about what it takes to live in proper virtue. This way they can reject sin and come closer to God over time through their virtue as the result of the help that God chose to give to them out of His mercy towards them.

Men do not necessarily need God to tell them about good and evil for them to know how to live in proper virtue or to avoid the contrary sins. Just as men can use their own natural reason to know about God's existence and some of His attributes, men can use their rational intellect to figure out right from wrong as well. Hence men can learn about proper virtue for the most part on their own if they are to live in this way. Thus they can come into the delight that is possible to them from the greatest possible good once they have obtained it. Yet they still need the help that God gives to men if they are to use their virtue to actually come closer to God in the end. If men live in proper virtue but do not intend the good works that they do for God's sake, they do not actually move closer to God. Hence virtue can potentially bring men closer to God, but it does not essentially do so in every case. Men need to intend the good works that they do for God's sake for them to actually come closer to God in the end. This means that God needs to show men the ways to come to Him if men are to use their virtue for that end. If men do not know that there is a way to God or what is the way to God, then they cannot intend their virtue as the means to come to God as the end. Hence they do not act for God despite their virtue. The men do the good works for their own selfish reasons rather than as a means to come closer to God in the hope of union with God in the state of beatitude. For this reason God chose to reveal Himself to men under the Old Law and the New Law. And the moral precepts contained in the Old Law and the New Law were intended for men to use the virtuous acts done in accord with what they had learned so that they could move closer to God in life. This is why it was necessary for there to be the Divine law in the first place. If God did not choose to give men the Divine law, men could not be saved.

Now it can be said that the different precepts that God gave to the Jews in the time of the Old Law were divided as being either moral, ceremonial, or juridical. The moral precepts are the ones that God gave to the Jews for the sake of their virtue. Thus the different moral precepts all concerned the obligations of men either to God or to their fellow men. Christ said that the greatest of all of the precepts is that men love God above all else and that they love God in the same way that they love their fellow man. Implicit in this command is also that men love themselves, since the love that they give to their fellow man is based on the love that they give to themselves. It can even be said that men should love themselves more than they love other men, since the image of a thing is less than the thing of which it is an image. So the love that men give to other men is based on the love that they give to themselves. Hence the proper order is that men love God above all else, followed by themselves, and then other men. This way men can seek out the greatest possible good in all cases for the sake of the delight that it can give them. God alone is essentially good, and love is the desire for the greatest possible good for its own sake. So when men love God above all else, they seek God for the way that God alone is essentially good. And they seek the good for themselves and for their fellow man relative to the essential goodness of God. Thus men should seek to come to God in their own lives, and at the same time, to bring other men to God for the sake of their benefit as well. This is how men fulfill the two parts of the greatest precept that God gave to the Jews and which Christ upheld for men under the New Law. Men seek the different created goods in life because those created goods can bring them closer to God in the end. The greater the created good itself, the closer it comes to God by its nature, as God alone is essentially good. Hence men ought to choose what is more like God over what is less like God, so that they can love God all the more through these acts in order to come closer to God in the possibility of being saved.

Now the moral precepts that God gave to the Jews can be summarized in the decalogue. These are the ten most important precepts that God gave to the Jews under the Old Law, which Christ said are likewise relevant in the time of the New Law. The decalogue forms the core of the Old Law for the Jewish people. Hence it is necessary to consider the ten different precepts contained in the decalogue. It can be said that each of the ten precepts of the decalogue mean more than what they directly state. There are broader implications that can be gathered from the things that God told the Jews when He gave them the decalogue. This broader understanding of these ten precepts can cover more of what men must do in order to act in proper virtue. Then they can use their virtue as the way to come to God.

The first precept says that the Jews are not to adore any other gods besides God Himself, and that they should not make any graven images. This means that men must make God the ultimate end of their being in the way that was said. Men seek the good for the sake of the delight that it can give them. As God alone is essentially good, men can receive from God in the state of beatitude a greater delight than they could ever receive from any created nature. So men ought to make God the ultimate end for their being in this way, so that all that they do is directed to God as the end for their existence. And God told the Jews that they could not make any graven images. This primarily means that the Jews could not adore false idols in the form of various material goods. But this can also be taken to mean that men should never make any created good to be their ultimate end either. Hence if a man seeks money in life as the ultimate end for his being, this is the sin of idolatry. He has taken the position of being the ultimate end and given it to the money that he seeks for himself, where God alone should be the ultimate end for men, since men can receive a greater delight from God than they could ever receive from the possession or the use of money. It is even possible that men can make errors in their minds about the nature of God and make the image in their minds to be their ultimate end rather than the God Who actually exists outside of their minds. This is another form of idolatry possible to men in life. Idolatry can be said to take place whenever men make any created good to be the ultimate end for their being. Since God made men to share in the essential goodness of His essence in beatitude, God prohibits men from making any lesser good to be their ultimate end instead of Himself. This is the first of the ten precepts of the decalogue and the one upon which all of the others depend, since all of the other precepts are intended as ways that men can move closer to God in life as the ultimate end for their being. This way they can come to be with God in the state of beatitude when they die.

The second precept of the decalogue says that men should not take the name of God in vain. This means that men ought to guard their speech in particular so that they show the proper respect to God and to their fellow man. If men use the name of God in vain, or speak vainly about other sacred things, they do not take those things seriously. Hence they do not give to God the love that God deserves from them because they consider these matters to be of some lesser importance. Thus God told the Jews not to speak of His name in vain. This is one of the ways that the Jews could learn to respect sacred things.

The third precept of the decalogue says that men should keep holy the Sabbath. God set apart one day out of every seven for men to give Him more adoration than they would give to Him on other days. Now there is nothing inherent in nature itself that says that men should give one day out of every seven to God, or that one time is inherently more sacred than another. This is all according to custom, and has no direct basis in natural law. But it is in accord with the proper order of nature that men give time to adore God apart from other times. If men seek to love God above all else, it is natural enough that they give a certain amount of time to focus more exclusively upon God. This can be done at other times, but it is in accord with God's will that one day out of every seven days is especially set apart for men to love and adore God. The broader implication of this precept is that men need to respect sacred things in general, since they are sacred because they are more closely related to God than other things. Hence if men have set apart certain times or objects for God, these things must be treated with respect as the way to show love to God to Whom they have a closer connection.

It is also evident from the first three precepts of the decalogue how they each give ways that men can better relate to God. While all three of the precepts share in common that they have God as their direct end, they differ from each other so that they refer to men being devoted to God according to thought, word, or deed. These are the three different ways that men can act, and these are the ways that men can use the three different kinds of acts to come closer to God in the hope of beatitude. Thus the men can direct themselves fully to God in thought, word, and deed for the sake of giving to God the good that God deserves from them, in return for the state of beatitude that God will give them when they die. The remaining five precepts of the decalogue all concern the ways that men relate to other men. So while the first three precepts have God as their direct end, the latter five have God as their indirect end and the good for oneself and one's fellow man as the direct end thereof. When men show love to their fellow man in these ways, they can use that love to come closer to God as well.

The fourth precept of the decalogue says that men should honor their father and mother. This is particularly the case because men receive all of the good that they have in life from their parents. They can never pay back an equal good to their parents for the good of their lives that they had received from them, but they can still show them love and respect for the way that their parents made the good possible to them in this way. That men should honor their father and mother also means that they need to respect authority figures for the sake of their own good. It is inevitably the case for all ordinary men that some men will know better than they do about certain things. So men should respect that other men may know better than they do and defer to the judgment of other men for the sake of their own good. It was already said that such obedience is in accord with the natural law, and it does not mean that the men abdicate their responsibility as beings endowed with a rational intellect and free will to find the good for them in accord with their conscience. This means that the men simply recognize that it is inevitable in some ways that other men know better than them, and that it thus makes sense to defer to the judgment of the other men. This is how it is proper for men to show respect to different authority figures for the sake of their own good. And the first authority figures that a man has in his life are his parents. Thus God told men that they should honor their father and mother.

The fifth precept of the decalogue is not to murder. This means that men are prohibited from the taking of an innocent human life. And this can mean more broadly that men should respect human life, since it is when men are alive that they have the capacity to come to God in the end. Life allows men to experience all of the other good things that are possible to them when the soul and body are united. Now virtue was said to mean that men seek the greatest possible good, and this includes that men seek the greatest possible good for their fellow man in imitation of how they seek the greatest possible good for themselves. Since it is better for men to live for the sake of the different goods that are possible to them in life, including the possibility to repent of their sins and come to God, it thus makes sense that men do all that they can to protect innocent human life. This means that not only can men kill other men when the other men are innocent, but they also cannot commit suicide, since this would be to deprive themselves of the other goods that are possible to them while they are alive. It would mean that the man who killed himself forfeited the goods that God had prepared for him while he was still alive. Since this would be an act of ingratitude to God in this manner, it is never permissible for men to kill other innocent men or to kill themselves either. Both of these acts are contrary to the fifth precept of the decalogue.

But at the same time, this does not rule out that it is in accord with proper virtue to use deadly force to protect the lives of innocent men. If a man kills a man in self-defense or defense of others, this does not contradict either the words or the spirit of the fifth precept of the decalogue. The man has actually preserved life through what he did when he killed the man who would have taken the lives of the innocent men, either himself or the lives of any other men that were at risk. It is also permissible for the temporal state to execute men when they have been justly convicted of crimes, since the common good of the whole society overrides the good for the individual man who is executed. The greater good is the good for the greater number of men, meaning the good for the whole society must be upheld if there is ever a conflict between the good for the society and the good of the individual. This means that the temporal state, which exists for the sake of upholding the temporal good for men, can execute men for crimes. And if the man executed for the crimes was guilty of murder, his execution would further uphold the importance of protecting human life, since the man who was executed failed to treat human life with the proper respect. As the punishment must be measured to the degree of the crime in order for the punishment to be in accord with justice, it can be said that the man who is executed in this way gave up his own right to live when he took the life of an innocent man. It can also be said that execution may justly be used for other serious crimes as well, where the nature of the crime would warrant execution as the only reasonable punishment. But it is up to the temporal state, as the authority charged with working for the sake of the common good, to decide which crimes to punish with execution.

The sixth precept of the decalogue tells men not to commit adultery. This can be taken to mean that men need to respect their nature as beings endowed with sexuality. Now the purpose of sex is procreation, so that the society itself can endure through the way that men and women are able to have children. The children can continue the society once they have become adults and the previous generation has come to an end. For the children to be raised in a proper environment so that they can become virtuous adults who will be an asset to their society, men and women should only engage in sex and the subsequent raising of the children when they are married to each other. The marriage contract provides a stable home life for them and their children. Hence any sexual activity outside of marriage is necessarily prohibited because such acts can result in children who will not be raised within the proper environment for the sake of their own benefit. It is likewise the case that any sexual acts devoid of the possibility of procreation are inherently immoral acts. A sinful or immoral act is an act that is lacking in due rectitude. This means that there is some element of the act that can conceivably be present but is not present at the time. Hence any such sexual act cannot be considered moral or acceptable in any degree or by any possible means. This means that not only are acts such as homosexuality or bestiality necessarily immoral, but any artificial acts that men and women can use to prevent conceiving a child in the sexual act within marriage are also immoral for the same reason. The sexual act must at least be open to procreation for it to be a moral act. Since marriage exists as a stable environment in which the parents can raise their children, any sexual act outside of marriage is immoral. This is the meaning of the sixth precept of the decalogue.

The seventh precept of the decalogue says that men cannot steal. This means that men have an obligation to protect the property rights that belong to men in society in order for them to survive and have some reasonable degree of delight. Now since the seventh precept necessarily concerns property rights, it must be said that a society that does not allow for or acknowledge the existence of private property would also be in violation of the seventh precept of the decalogue as well. A human society can only survive and flourish if it acknowledges the natural right of men to own private property for their own sake and for the sake of those who are close to them. And the recognition that the society itself ought to give to the existence and necessity of private property also means that the temporal state ought to create economic conditions that conduce to as many men as possible owning and maintaining their own private property. A society that does not maintain private property as one of its goals cannot expect to survive, to thrive, or to do justice for the men within the society. Hence it belongs to both the individual men in the society and to the temporal state that is set over the society to protect property rights for men. It is unjust for a man to take the property of another man without the other man's consent and without giving anything back to him in return, since this means that the man who took the property prevents the other man from using the property taken for his own good. Hence this is contrary to the greatest possible good for the other man, which the man must uphold in order for him to remain in proper virtue. But there is also the case that men can take private property from other men in certain extreme cases, such as if a man is starving and he steals some food to survive. The greater good is that the one man does not starve compared to the man himself protecting the property rights of the other man by not stealing the food. The greater good must always be the end for which the men act. If there is a greater good at stake, men can violate the natural right of private property in this way. But to do so when there is no greater good at stake is immoral, regardless of whether it is an individual man taking the private property for his own use or if it is the temporal state doing the same for some alleged common good.

The eighth precept of the decalogue is that men should not bear false witness against each other. This means that men cannot lie, where a lie is defined as a statement that contradicts what the man himself knows in his mind. Hence men must speak the truth to each other, since if the other men know the truth, they can use it to find the greatest possible good in the given case in order for them to delight in the good once it has been obtained. Thus the truth leads men to the delight that is possible to them in the given case. For men to speak the truth to each other is to help the other men find the good that is possible to them as well. Thus men work for the good of the other men when they refuse to speak lies to them concerning what they know about different things. Yet it might be the case that a man might ask something of another man, when the first man has the intention of using the truth to do some evil. The first man might ask about the location of another man so that he can unjustly harm the other man when he finds him. If the man asked knows that the other man will use or is likely to use the information to unjustly harm the other man, it is permissible for him to lie to the other man about the location of the man who would otherwise suffer from some kind of unjust harm. The end for which men ought to tell the truth is so that other men can use the truth for the sake of the greater good. So if the men who know the truth intend not to use it for the sake of the greater good, then the end for which the truth is the means does not exist. The means exist for the sake of the end. So if the end which ought to be the greater good is not upheld in the given case, there is no reason for the means either, meaning that the man who was asked has no reason to tell the truth to the other man. This can likewise be justified because the greatest possible good is the proper end of all virtue. Hence if a man does not use the truth for the greatest possible good, which is the way that the truth ought to be used, then other men can lie to that man in order to uphold the greatest possible good in the given case. This is likewise an act of justice to the man whom the lie is intended to protect, since the man would be unjustly harmed if the one man told the truth to the other man about his location. So while men have an obligation to tell the truth to other men for the sake of the greatest possible good for the other men, if that good is not sought through the truth once it is known, it is permissible to lie for the sake of the greater good that must be upheld in accord with proper virtue. But absent such extreme cases, men have an obligation to tell each other the truth for the sake of upholding the greatest possible good for their fellow man as much as this is possible.

The ninth precept of the decalogue is that a man should not desire his neighbor's wife. This means that a man should respect his relation both to his own wife and to the other people around him. Thus he should not seek to use his neighbor's wife for the sake of his own sexual delight, even if he did not actually try to have sex with her. Christ said that if a man so much as looks at a woman who is not his wife with a sexual desire, this is just as evil as if he had actually committed adultery with her. This is because the man who acts in this way shows that he would have committed adultery with the other woman if this was possible to him. While he did not do the evil act, his will was still inclined to evil so that he would have done it if this was possible to him. Since his will is still set on evil, he can be punished for the evil that he desired much in the same way as if he actually did the evil act itself.

The tenth precept of the decalogue is that a man should not desire his neighbor's goods. This means that he is content with his own possessions and does not seek to have more than he needs for his survival or delight. It is possible for a man to desire the material goods of his fellow man without this necessarily being sinful. It only becomes a sin when the man regrets that his fellow man has these material goods while he does not possess them. This means that the man fails to desire the good for his fellow man by the way that he desires that his fellow man not have those same goods. Thus he does not have the proper desire for the greatest possible good for his fellow man, which is how this is a sin.

From what has been said, it is evident that there is an order among the ten precepts of the decalogue. The first three precepts all concern God as the direct end for men, while the latter five precepts concern men as the direct end and God as the indirect end. It can also be said that the first three precepts mean that God gets what He deserves from men in thought, word, and deed. This is how these three are distinct from each other. For the five precepts that concern the good for one's fellow man, the first three precepts concern deeds, the next precept concerns words, and the final two precepts concern thoughts. For the first three precepts which concern deeds, they respectively involve a man's life, his family, and his material property. For the last two precepts, they respectively concern what the man owes to other men concerning their families and their material property.

All ten of the precepts contained in the decalogue can be taken to refer to greater goods beyond those that are apparent within the words themselves that God gave to the Jews under the Old Law. There are much broader implications for all of them concerning the ways that men can work for the sake of the greatest possible good, either relative to God as the direct end or to his fellow man as the indirect end. It is also evident that all ten of these precepts are derived from the natural law. This is also the case for the first three precepts which exclusively concern God. It was said that men can know about God through the power of their own natural reason, meaning that what men owe to God for Who He is concerns the natural law in this way, even though God Who is above all of nature is the proper end for all of them. These precepts are all concerned with justice as one of the cardinal virtues rather than with any of the three theological virtues. And it is the theological virtues that God must infuse into men for them to be saved, while the cardinal virtues are possible to men according to their own natural abilities.

After the moral precepts that gave to the Jews in the time of the Old Law, it is necessary to consider the ceremonial precepts. God gave these precepts to the Jews so that they could properly adore God. Now there were many different ceremonial precepts that the Jews had to observe when they gave their adoration to God. It is not necessary to consider all of them individually. But it may be said that the ceremonial precepts in general were necessary for men to relate more directly to God. Men can love God through all that they do when they act in accord with proper virtue. Virtue is for the sake of the greatest possible good in every case, and God alone is essentially good because being is the same thing as goodness and the Divine essence is existence Itself. Hence men can direct all of their good works to God for His sake, in the hope that they will eventually be saved. But because men are to love

God above all else, it is consistent with the love that men owe to God that they do certain things exclusively for God's sake. Thus they need some ways to direct the mind and the will to God alone in order to properly give to God the love that God deserves from them. Since men are composed of soul and body, and these two parts of men are naturally united, it stands to reason that men would use certain bodily acts and even material goods as the way to show that they love God.

Now God in His essence is absolutely perfect, meaning that He lacks nothing at all from His very being. So God does not need any good things that men can give to Him, not even the love that men seek to provide to God for the sake of His own essential goodness. Much less does God need the bodily observances or the material goods that they involve that men offer to Him for the sake of His own delight. God's own essence is the sole and perfect source of His own delight. But since men are both soul and body, it is proper that men give adoration to God in ways that conduce to their own nature. Hence Christ said that God made the Sabbath for man rather than man for the Sabbath. Men need to give their adoration to God for their own sake at the same time that they do this for God's sake. God does not need the adoration that men give to Him in the way that men to give the adoration to God. Since men thus need the adoration for their own good, they must relate to God in this way. And the different ceremonial precepts that God gave to the Jews in the time of the Old Law governed the ways that the Jews should exclusively relate to God for the sake of their own good.

It is also the case that the ceremonial precepts that God gave to the Jews under the Old Law were mostly superseded by the New Law. This is because one of the other reasons that God gave the Jews their ceremonial precepts under the Old Law was so that they could prefigure Christ Whom they adored by those precepts in the time preceding the First Coming. The ceremonial precepts that God gave to the Jews in the time of the Old Law were meant to teach the Jews about Christ through the various symbols that were in them. So when Christ came to earth at the time of the First Coming, so that men could know Christ in reality in the way that this was not also possible in the time of the Old Law, it was no longer necessary or possible for the Jews to adore Christ in figure any longer. Men were able to adore Christ in reality because they now knew Him a way that this was not previously possible. Hence the ceremonial precepts of the Old Law were mostly superseded by the New Law that Christ had given to fallen men at the First Coming.

It was proper that there were many different ceremonial precepts that the Jews were required to observe in the time of the Old Law. The different precepts all involved some symbolism of what was to come. They all looked forward to the way that Christ would come to save fallen men at the time of the First Coming. While it is not possible here to consider each of the different ways that the precepts led the Jews adore Christ in the time of the Old Law, it is still necessary to consider the three different kinds of ceremonial precepts that God gave to the Jews under the Old Law for their benefit. The four different kinds of ceremonial precepts that God gave to the Jews were the sacrifices, sacraments, sacramentals, and observances.

First, the many different animal sacrifices that the Jews offered to God in the time of the Old Law were so that the Jews could give some good to God. Hence the Jews offered the best of the animals that they possessed to God in the Temple as their sacrifices. They always worked to offer the best that they had to God as the way to show that they loved God more than the created goods that they could get from the animals that they instead offered to God. This was a way for them to show their love for God, meaning that this was an act of justice. The Jews thereby recognized that God alone is essentially good and that He is worthy of love above all else. While no ordinary man can ever give to God a good that is commensurate with the infinite goodness of God, it is still in accord with justice that men offer the best of the goods that they have to God for the sake of His own essential goodness. Since God alone is perfectly just, God will give some good back to men for the goods that they were willing to offer to Him. This was one of the lessons that God sought to teach the Jews in the time of the Old Law by the different animals that they offered to Him in the Temple. But the most important lesson that God sought to teach the Jews through the animal sacrifices is how Christ would offer Himself as God and man on the Cross so that fallen men could be saved in the end. This way men could receive the Divine grace and virtue from Christ on the Cross in order for them to be saved when they die. Thus men can come to be with God in the state of beatitude.

Second, there were the sacraments. These were intended for the Jews for them to understand how the seven sacraments that Christ and the apostles gave to the Church on earth would sanctify men under the New Law by allowing men to unite themselves to Christ on the Cross in order for them to be saved when they die. Hence God gave the Jews under the Old Law their sacraments to prefigure the sacraments of the New

Law. But while the seven sacraments of the New Law offer the reality of the Divine grace and virtue to men for them to be saved, the sacraments of the Old Law only offered the men the figure of the Divine grace and virtue. As the Jews adored Christ in figure under the Old Law, they only received the figure of the Divine grace and virtue from Christ at the same time. Christ gave the Jews under the Old Law the figure of the Divine grace and virtue for the way that they adored Him in figure. This would prepare them to better understand the ways that the reality of the Divine grace and virtue would work for the faithful in the Church on earth under the New Law. So in the same way that the seven sacraments of the Church on earth sanctify the faithful in reality, the sacraments of the Jews in the time of the Old Law sanctified them in figure.

Third, there were the sacramentals that the Jews used in their rites under the Old Law. It was said that since God made men as both soul and body, and these two parts of men work together for the good of the man himself, it thus makes sense that men would use material things in order for them to better serve God. This does not mean that God needs any such things, but they can help men to better dispose themselves before God in order for them to give to God the love that God ought to receive from men for the way that He alone is essentially good. Hence the value of such sacramentals is not for what they are within themselves, but for what they represent. Christ commended Mary for giving Him the expensive oil though this was a material good. Christ was not so much concerned with the expensive oil that He had received, but with the way that Mary showed Him that she loved Him when she purchased the oil to give to Him. This was the significance of that event. And when Christ consented to receive the expensive oil, even over the protests of the apostles about the ways that the money for the oil could have been used, Christ showed that it is possible for men to use material goods as a way to show their love for God. This is also in the way that the psalmist said that God told men to rend their hearts rather than their garments. It was not so much the ritual tearing of the clothing that mattered to God, but that the men were sorry for the sins that they had committed against God and that they would seek to come into His grace and virtue in order for them to love Him more. So while the material goods that men use to adore God do not have any inherent value of their own, their value is that they can help to dispose men to properly relate to God with and through such items. Men can thus give to God the love and adoration that He deserves from them for His essential goodness.

Fourth, there were the observances that God had imposed upon the Jews in the time of the Old Law. These regulated the ways that the Jews interacted with each other and with the other nations of the earth. The observances allowed the Jews to remember God even when they were not directly offering their sacrifices to God or seeking to come closer to Him by the sacraments that God had given to them for that purpose. This way the Jews could effectively consecrate their other acts to God in their lives, so that they could recall God above all else as the one for Whom they should seek to do their good works. As with the other things that the Jews had offered to God, the virtue of the observances was not so much that the Jews gave a particular good to God, but that it was to God to Whom they gave the good that was done. God did not need the goods that they offered to Him by their observances, but they observed these things for the sake of their own good and because God deserved some good from them.

This is the significance of the ceremonial precepts that God imposed upon the Jews in the time of the Old Law for the sake of their benefit. All of them concern Christ in some way, since the Jews under the Old Law looked forward to the First Coming. But the men who live in the time since the First Coming do not look forward to this event in the way that the Jews did, meaning that most of the ceremonial precepts that God gave to the Jews were superseded when Christ came to save men at the time of the First Coming. Christ offered men the reality where the Jews only had the figure thereof. The need for the figure of the Divine grace and virtue was definitively superseded by Christ giving men the reality of the Divine grace and virtue itself from the Cross by the way that He chose to die on the Cross and then rise from the dead for that purpose.

Among the different kinds of precepts that God gave to the Jews in the time of the Old Law was the juridical precepts. These rules were meant to govern the ways that the Jews interacted with other people. Like much of the rest of what God gave to the Jews in the time of the Old Law, this was intended to prefigure what was to come in the New Law. So these precepts would also eventually be superseded in the time of Christ. God told the Jews through the juridical precepts how they were to act in four different ways. They covered how the rulers of the Jewish society were to treat the ordinary people whom they ruled as well as the converse, the ways that the individual Jews in their own society were to interact with each other, the ways that the Jews were supposed to interact with their own families, and the ways that the Jews were to interact with the Gentiles.

Hence these different rules were meant to uphold an orderly human society for the Jews in the time of the Old Law. Now since much of what applied for the Jews in the time of the Old Law does not also strictly apply to the faithful in the Church on earth, it can be said that many of these precepts were only intended for the Jews in their time rather than for the faithful under the New Law.

Taken as a whole, the precepts of the Old Law were a considerable burden for the Jews to observe in their time. The precepts that bind the faithful in the Church on earth under the New Law are not as many or as severe as the ones that God had imposed upon the Jews. Christ Himself said the same when He stated that His yoke is easy and His burden is light. Christ thus compared the precepts that He gave to the faithful in the Church on earth under the New Law to what God had given to the Jews under the Old Law. But it makes sense that God imposed the more difficult burden on the Jews under the Old Law. The Old Law was preparatory as the way for mankind to eventually receive Christ at the time of the First Coming, and the preparation for a thing is often more difficult than the actual thing itself. So for men to better be prepared to adore Christ in reality in the time of the New Law, God made the Old Law a much greater burden for men. Some of the precepts that bound the Jews under the Old Law, such as the decalogue, are still as relevant to the faithful in the Church on earth under the New Law as they were to the Jews under the Old Law. But most of the precepts of the Old Law have been replaced by the reality that they were meant to symbolize, and the reality in the New Law is a lesser burden than the figure of the reality had been under the Old Law.

There were also some precepts where Christ Himself made things more difficult for the faithful than they had been for the Jews. Thus Christ told the faithful that divorce is never allowed under the New Law, since God had permitted divorce under the Old Law as a concession to the Jews. But since Christ now called men to spiritual and moral perfection, this would no longer be the case. Hence marriage exists until the time of death for one or both of the spouses. Christ also imposed a heavier burden under the New Law when He told the faithful that they should love even their enemies. On the occasions when Christ imposed a heavier burden on men compared to the Old Law, it was because God chose in those cases to move men from a lesser to a greater degree of perfection. This is much in the way that the Old Law itself relates to the New Law, even though the Old Law was admittedly the heavier burden for men to observe.

God had imposed upon the Jews a difficult burden with the Old Law. Hence it perhaps is understandable to some degree that the Jews had repeatedly transgressed the precepts that God had given to them. This happened in four ways. First, the Jews often relapsed back into the sin of idolatry, where they adopted the different pagan gods of the nations around them and gave their adoration to these gods rather than to the true God Who had delivered them from Egypt and Who had given them many good things. Now God knew from the beginning that the Jews would behave in this way despite how they were His chosen people. Yet God continued to lead the Jews under the Old Law despite the ways that they were repeatedly ungrateful to Him. Second, the Jews often followed the Old Law not so much for them to give the love to God that God had deserved from them, but for the sake of the different rites themselves. The Jews thought that the rites that God had given to them had some inherent value of their own rather than the way that God told them to do these things for His sake out of the love that they should have had for Him. This is one of the ways that they failed to act in the way that God had intended for the sake of their own good. Third, the Jews often used clever interpretations to circumvent the observance of the rites that God had imposed upon them under the

Old Law. If a particular observance was too difficult for them to handle, they would defy the observance itself yet still follow some technicality in order to claim that they obeyed the particular precept of the Old Law. This is why St. Paul the Apostle said that the letter kills but the spirit gives life. The Jews followed the letter of the Old Law but did not observe the spirit of what was intended by the letter. Fourth, rather than submit to God in humility, the Jews would sometimes become proud about the ways that they had observed the Old Law, or how God had given the Old Law to them and not to any of the other nations of the earth. This was despite how God said that He chose the Jews to be His people because they were not one of the great nations of the earth in their time.

       Now while the Jews under the Old Law had offended God in these ways, it is also the case that the faithful in the Church on earth under the New Law can fall into the same offenses against God if they are not also careful. The New Law can become the source of such difficulty for men just as the Old Law did for the Jews in their time. This does not mean that there was anything necessarily lacking to either the Old Law or the New Law. Both of them come from God and both of them are good each in their own way. They are what God had intended for their respective times in the economy of human salvation. But men can misuse or abuse the good things that God has given them so that those things become an occasion for sin. This is the case even with the observance of the Divine law that God gave to men for men to be saved.

Yet God allows evil to exist in order to bring some good even out of evil. And it can be said that the Jews under the Old Law can be interpreted in four different ways. First, this can refer to the Jews themselves who actually transgressed the Divine will many times throughout the course of their history under the Old Law. Second, this can refer to the way that the Church on earth will also fall into some corruption in the time of the New Law, which Christ said when He gave the Church on earth the parable of the wheat and the cockle growing together in the field. Third, this can refer to how individual men lapse back into sin despite the ways that they may have received the Divine grace and virtue from Christ. The Divine grace and virtue that men receive under the New Law is not irresistible and can be lost even after men had internally accepted it for their own benefit. Fourth, this can refer to all of fallen mankind in general, because not only individual men but whole societies can fall into grave sins and abandon their faith in God.

In the same way that God remained with the Jews under the Old Law despite all of the different ways that the Jews had sinned against Him, God never abandons the Church on earth, individual men in life, or fallen mankind in general despite all of the sins and the corruption that take place. Since men in life can always repent of their sins and become good when they were formerly evil, God never abandons men in life. The way that God remained with the Jews despite how they had behaved in the time of the Old Law reveals more of God's own essential goodness to men in these other cases as well. This is an example of how God allows evil to exist in order to bring some good even out of evil. It is evil that the Jews or the different men in these other cases commit their sins against God, but then God uses these sins to show men more of His mercy. When the men better know the Divine mercy to them despite all of the ways that they had sinned against God, they can better love God because they see more of His essential goodness.

When the Jews had repeatedly fallen into different sins under the Old Law, God chose to deal with these matters in two ways. First, God would punish the Jews for the sins that they had committed. Hence after the two Jewish kingdoms had repeatedly fallen into sin, God allowed them to be conquered and for the Jews themselves to be sent into exile in Babylon for a generation. This was one of the greater punishments that God sent to the Jews for their sins. From the time that the two Jewish kingdoms were destroyed, the Jews would never again under the Old Law have their own independent state as they formerly did. God took away the good from them because they did not deserve it due to their many sins against Him. And when God allowed the Jews to suffer from such punishments under the Old Law, He revealed to them more of His justice. God was still with the Jews even though they had sinned. God never abandoned them throughout the time of the Old Law, just as He never gives up on men in life despite the sins by which many men have rejected Him. But while God is good to men in this way and He is merciful to men at other times, God still exacts His justice against sinful men for the sake of their own good. In this case, as in the other cases when God punishes men in life, the punishment that God gives to men is meant to get them to repent of their sins and come into proper virtue. This way the men can avoid having to suffer in the future from more punishments that they would justly bring upon themselves if they were to commit more sins against God. And in the event that they still commit more sins despite how God had already punished them, the punishments that God sends them in life can serve as a warning to them of the much worse suffering that He will allow them to receive in hell if they do not repent while they are alive repentance is still possible to them. This was one of God's responses to the Jews for their sins under the Old Law, and it also applies to the sinners in other times and places as well.

Second, when the Jews had fallen back into sin at various times under the Old Law, God sent the different prophets to the Jews to call them to repent of their sins and to properly observe the Old Law that God had given to them for their own good. In many cases the prophets under the Old Law did not convince many men from among the Jews to return to God. Christ remarked at the time of the First Coming how the Jews had notoriously rejected many of the prophets that God sent to them in the time of the Old Law. Christ said that it made sense that the Jews would reject Him as well even though He is the promised Redeemer Whom they had already adored in figure under the Old Law. But regardless of the reception that the Jews under the Old Law gave to the prophets, it was the case that the prophets for the most part all engaged in two related functions. First, they directed the Jews back to the Old Law which God had given to Moses when God led the Jews from Egypt and into the promised land. Second, they looked forward to the First Coming, when God would become man as Christ, and when Christ would suffer on the Cross and then rise from the dead as the way to save fallen men. The prophets both looked back to Moses and ahead to Christ. Since the Old Law prefigured Christ and the New Law that Christ gives to men for them to be saved, to look back to Moses was another way for the Jews to look ahead to Christ at the time of the First Coming.

CHAPTER IV.
THE NEW LAW

The New Law that God gave to mankind began at the time of the First Coming. God became man as Christ and Christ chose to suffer and die on the Cross and then rise from the dead as the way for men to receive the Divine grace and virtue that they need to be saved. As Christ is both God and man in the one hypostasis, Christ is the fulfillment of the Divine revelation that began in the time of Abraham at the beginning of the Old Law. As God gave men the Divine law in both the Old Law and the New Law to bring men to be with Him in the state of beatitude, it makes sense that God Himself Who became man as Christ would be the fulfillment of what God had revealed to men for them to be saved.

Now it is necessary to understand what is meant when it is said that Christ is both God and man in the one hypostasis. The Son, as the second person of the Trinity, chose to unite Himself to the human nature that was created, so that the hypostasis formed at the same time of the human nature contains both the Son and the human nature itself. This is how Christ is both God and man. There are three things to be considered in

Christ. There is the Divine nature, the human nature, and the one hypostasis Which contains both of these two natures. The hypostasis of a thing is defined as this thing of this nature rather than that thing of this nature. So two men are of the same essence, that of men, while one man is a different hypostasis from the other man. Thus there are two different hypostases, one for each man, while both of the men are of the same essence. So when it is said that Christ is both God and man in the one hypostasis, it belongs to Christ as this one hypostasis to be both God and man. And insofar as Christ is God, it is the Son as the second person of the Trinity Who united Himself to the human nature at the time that the human nature was conceived within Mary. Insofar as Christ is a man, Christ is fully man, meaning that Christ's humanity is composed of both soul and body. Christ is not a human body animated by the Son in place of a human soul, because this would mean that Christ is not fully man as well as fully God. So Christ in His human nature has both a human soul and body. This is the way that Christ is fully man in all things except for sin, where sin is not essential to human nature as such.

Since Christ is both God and man in the one hypostasis, this means that Christ is both uncreated and created. As Christ is fully God, the Divine nature in Christ is uncreated. This can be said for all three of the Divine persons because the processions in God take place in eternity. So while the Son comes forth from the Father and the Holy Spirit from the Father and the Son, there was never a time when any of the Divine persons did not exist. They always proceed just as They have always been. And since Christ is truly God, this means that the Son with Christ is uncreated. But since Christ is truly a man as well, this means that Christ's human nature is indeed created, so that it did not exist before Christ was conceived within Mary by the power of the Holy Spirit. This means that Christ as a man did not exist forever, but rather that His human nature began to be at the time that He was conceived within Mary. And since the hypostasis of a thing depends upon the essence of the thing to be what it is, it can thus be said that the one hypostasis Who is Christ began to be in time. This is necessarily the case because Christ as a man began to be in time, and the one hypostasis Who is Christ depends as much upon the human nature as It depends upon the Divine nature for Christ to be Who He is.

    Hence the one hypostasis did not exist at all before the human nature of Christ. This would mean that Christ was not necessarily a man as well as God, which would make no sense. Both of the natures within the one hypostasis must be present if Christ is to be Who He is. So before

Christ was conceived within Mary, there was no Christ as God made man. There is the eternal Son, but the Son had not yet united Himself to the human nature until the time when Christ was conceived by the Holy Spirit. Christ also did not exist as a man before becoming God. Christ is both God and man as Who He is, meaning that Christ is not a man who was later united to the Son within the one hypostasis. This would mean that the hypostasis that came into being in this way was not the same as the hypostasis before the union of the two natures. Hence Christ would not have been the same person before and after this event, which makes no sense. For Christ to be Christ, He is necessarily God and man within the one hypostasis.

It is necessarily the case that Christ is both God and man in the one hypostasis in this way if Christ's sacrifice of Himself on the Cross is to be efficacious to save fallen men. Christ is truly God, and God alone can bring being out of non-being because His essence is existence Itself. This means that God alone can forgive the sins of fallen men with the infusion of the Divine grace and virtue. Sin is when men choose a lesser good over the greatest possible good in the given case. Hence the end of sin lacks some possible good, meaning that the sin lacks some possible good as well, since things are defined by their ends. This also means that the sinner lacks some of the possible good from within himself for the lack of the possible good to come from him in this manner, since the effect always resembles the cause in order for it to be the effect of that cause. Thus the sinner lacks some possible good from within himself, which is evident from the way that the man had committed the sin in the first place. And since God alone can bring being out of non-being, this means that God alone can restore men to the being of the Divine grace and virtue when this was lacking to them because of sin. As Christ is truly God, this means that Christ can give men the Divine grace and virtue that they need for them to be saved when they die. And Christ chose to give men the Divine grace and virtue by the way that He died on the Cross and then rose from the dead.

It is equally necessary that Christ is truly a man in order for Christ's death on the Cross to bring men into the Divine grace and virtue from their former state of sin. Christ as a man was able to represent fallen men back to God in order to pay the debt of love that fallen men owed to God for their sins. It was said that men failed to love God when they had committed their sins against Him. So God became man as Christ, and then Christ died on the Cross and then rose from the dead to give back to God the love that God should have received from fallen men in the first place. This means that Christ did justice to God on behalf of fallen men when Christ died on the Cross and then rose from the dead. So when fallen men choose to unite themselves to Christ on the Cross for them to receive the Divine grace and virtue, they do their own justice to God through Christ. This enables them to be saved when they die.

    It can also be said that since Christ as both God and man offered Himself as both God and man back to God from the Cross, that Christ did perfect justice to God. The essential goodness of the Divine essence is infinite while all created natures are finite. All created natures are composed of matter and form. The matter of a thing is the potentiality and the form is the actuality. The mater and form limit the nature of the thing that is composed of matter and form. The matter limits what the form can become, and the form reduces the matter from many possibilities to one actual thing. This is how all things composed of matter and form are necessarily finite. But God alone is pure form because the potentiality of a thing is determined by what caused it. And God has no cause because He is the first cause, meaning that He has no potentiality either, which is how He is pure form. Since God alone is pure form without any matter, this means that His essence is infinite. And an infinite good cannot come from a finite being. The effect must be in the cause in order for it to be the effect of that cause, meaning that the infinite good would have to be in the finite being in order to come from it. But the infinite cannot be in the finite because this would be to impose limits on what has no limits. So it is impossible for an infinite good to come from a finite being. This means that no created nature could ever do perfect justice to God of his own accord because he cannot be the cause of an infinite good. Yet since Christ is both God and man in the one hypostasis, and Christ gave God back to God from the Cross, Christ gave an infinite good back to an infinite good, meaning that Christ in this manner was able to give God as much of the good that God deserves for the way that God alone is infinitely good. Thus when men choose of their own accord to unite themselves to Christ on the Cross, they can also do perfect justice to God through Christ. This means that they can merit to come to God in the state of beatitude, since they were able with the help of Christ to give an infinite good back to God for the sake of God's own infinite goodness. This is clear from what was said.

These are the ways that Christ made it possible for men to be saved when they die. Now when men unite themselves to Christ on the Cross, they do this in order for them to receive the Divine grace and virtue that Christ had made possible to men in this way. It was said that all of the Divine grace and virtue that comes to men for them to be saved comes from Christ on the Cross. Hence Christ is the only way for men to come to God in the state of beatitude when they die. When men unite themselves to Christ on the Cross, they receive the Divine grace and virtue. Grace is God's good favor which comes to the men who do His will. And virtue was said to be the desire for the greatest possible good in every case. It is above all else a desire for God because of the way that God alone is essentially good, as being is the same thing as goodness and the Divine essence is existence Itself. Now God gives men the three theological virtues in particular together with His grace when they choose to unite themselves to Christ on the Cross. The three theological virtues are so called because God alone is the direct end for all of them. Men can acquire the cardinal virtues on their own, since their direct end is created goods, while God is only the indirect end thereof, as He alone is essentially good. But men can only use the cardinal virtues to come closer to God in life when they do this by means of the three theological virtues. This is how it is possible for men to come to be with God in the state of beatitude when they die.

Since God is the direct end of the theological virtues, so that men can only come closer to God by means of the three theological virtues, it is necessarily the case that men can only have the three theological virtues if God gives them to men for the men to be saved. God is above all of His creation because He alone is the first cause of all other things that exist, and the cause of a thing being such is yet more so. Nothing can rise above itself by its own power. It can only come to things at its own level or beneath it. Hence for men to come to God in any degree means that men need the help that God alone can give them by His grace and virtue. And God gives all of the grace and virtue that He offers to men from Christ on the Cross. In this way it can be said that God becoming man as Christ to save men would still have been necessary even if men had not sinned, since men in the state of the original grace and virtue in which God had made them still could not rise above their level any more than men in the fallen state. But God still allowed the first men to commit the original sin which caused the Fall, since this would enable men to learn the difference between good and evil, so that they could choose the good over the evil and become the proximate cause of the good that they did. Thus they could receive a greater reward from God for the good that they did in this manner.

    Hence men need the Divine grace and virtue that God gives to men in order for them to be saved. And Christ offers the Divine grace and virtue to all men from the Cross. Thus any man who so desires can receive the Divine grace and virtue from Christ on the Cross in the possibility that he may be saved when he dies. But this of itself does not mean that all men as such will receive the Divine grace and virtue for them to be saved when they die. Two things must concur in this way for men to actually be saved. First, God must move the man externally by the Divine grace and virtue itself. Second, the man must choose to accept the Divine grace and virtue internally in order for him to be saved. When the man internally accepts the Divine grace and virtue that God had offered to him, so that he dies in that state, he can come to be with God in the state of beatitude. Now God can offer men the Divine grace and virtue without the men accepting the same internally. God gave men their free will, which means that men retain the ability to act contrary to the good that God had intended them to do by their free will. So while God externally moves men by the Divine grace and virtue, this does not mean that the men will necessarily accept it internally for them to be saved. The Divine grace and virtue that God offers to men is not irresistible.

Even if the men internally accepted the Divine grace and virtue at one time in their lives, they can still reject the same at a later time and lose what God had given to them. Men are not confirmed in either good or evil while they live. This only happens when they die and the soul and body separate from each other. Men receive all of their information about the created world from the external senses of the body, which deliver their new information to the rational intellect that derives from the soul. But when men die, the soul and body separate from each other, meaning that the rational intellect with the soul no longer has the same access that it once did to the new information from the external senses of the body. And new information is needed for men to change back and forth from either good or evil to the converse. This means that the separated soul is confirmed in the state of either good or evil in which the man had died. But when the men are still alive, they can still receive the new information that enables them to go back and forth from either good or evil to the converse. This means that good men can become evil by losing the grace and virtue that God gave them, while evil men can repent of their sins and become good by receiving the Divine grace and virtue. So men have to retain the Divine grace and virtue that they received once they internally accepted it in order for them to be saved when they die. Thus they can come to be with God in the state of beatitude. It is actually better that men in life retain their ability to lose the Divine grace and virtue once they have received it because this means that they have to do more of the good to remain in that state. Hence they can merit more from God when they keep the Divine grace and virtue that God gave to them, meaning that God can eventually give them a greater reward in the end for the sake of their greater merit.

Thus it is evident that men must choose to internally accept the Divine grace and virtue if they are to die in that state and come to be with God in the state of beatitude. If the men reject the external offer of the Divine grace and virtue that God made to them, they cannot be saved in the end. God knows all things that can possibly be known, meaning that God knows when He offers the Divine grace and virtue to some men that the external offer made will be rejected. Why God does this cannot be said. But since God does all that He does for the sake of the greatest possible good in every case, there must be some good that comes from God externally offering the Divine grace and virtue to men who reject it. Otherwise there would be no purpose for this to take place, and God does nothing without purpose.

It is also possible that while God makes the Divine grace and virtue possible to all men as such, He may not directly make the external offer of the Divine grace and virtue to some men for them to be saved. Some men might even seek the help that God gives to men in this way, but they do not receive the offer in the first place. In which case these men may receive the Divine grace by extraordinary means that enable them to be saved in the end. It would be unjust for God to condemn these men for the sake of what was outside of their control. So while some men may want to believe but God has not given them the faith, this does not preclude that God may still give the men the Divine grace because they were properly disposed to receive it. They were able to do the good as much as this was possible to them in their state, taking into account that God did not externally offer them the Divine grace and virtue in the ordinary way.

The converse is also the case in some way. God can and does give the Divine grace and virtue to some men whom He did not externally move by the Divine grace and virtue in the first place. Hence men can receive the Divine grace and virtue in life even if God did not choose to move them for that purpose. The men can seek the Divine grace and virtue on their own in some cases, and God will give it to them. But since God did not externally move them to internally accept the Divine grace and virtue, they will not endure in the Divine grace and virtue until death, meaning that they are still sent to hell when they die.

Thus God did not choose them for the state of beatitude if they did not make it to God in the state of beatitude. While these men are not saved in the end, they can still internally accept the Divine grace and virtue, since if God was to withhold it from them for the sake of future sins that they would commit, God would be punishing the men for what had yet to take place. Since this is unjust, and God alone is perfectly just, God does not act in this manner. So men who are not saved can internally receive the Divine grace and virtue by their free will without God externally moving them in this way, meaning that despite the way that they actually internally received the Divine grace and virtue, they do not come to be with God in the state of beatitude. Thus they were not saved regardless of what happened to them in life.

From what has been said, it is clear that there are many different ways that God and man can relate regarding the Divine grace and virtue. If a man was in the Divine grace and virtue in life but he does not make it to God in the state of beatitude, the man was not predestined by God for beatitude. The Divine will is always fulfilled because it takes a greater power to overcome a lesser one, and there is no power greater than that of God. Hence what God wills for things will always certainly take place as God willed it. So if God had willed that men come to be with Him in the state of beatitude, the men will certainly make it there. But if the men are not saved, then God did not predestine the men from eternity for the state of beatitude with Him when they had died. Thus the men who are in the Divine grace and virtue in life but who are not saved are present in the book of life by grace alone, while the predestined are present in the book of life by both grace and election. Both grace and election are necessary for the men to be saved when they die. This means that God moves the men externally by the Divine grace and virtue and that the men internally accept the same so that they die within it. This is how they can come to be with God in the state of beatitude.

The way that God externally moves men by the Divine grace and virtue for the men to internally accept the same is the process of justification. Men are justified when it is possible for them to come to God in beatitude. This was said to take place through the concurrence of both the Divine will and the man's own free will at the same time. God must save them and the men must work with God for them to be saved. This entire process can be described as justice within the context of mercy. It was said that God did not have to save any men at all regardless of whether the men had fallen or had remained in the state of the original grace and virtue in which God had made them. God saved men out of His own abundant mercy. Since men had indeed fallen, God would have been perfectly justified in sending all fallen men to hell for the sins that they had committed against Him, both for the original sin and the personal sins that they had committed consequent upon the original sin. But God knew that He could bring about some greater good for men if He was merciful to them and chose to save some men despite how they had sinned against Him. This is how God saving men is an act of mercy to men. But the men must also merit from God for them to internally accept the Divine grace and virtue, meaning that God does justice to men when they merit their beatitude from God using the help that God offers to them by His mercy. Thus it can be said that God saving men is the work of God's justice within the context of His mercy. This enables men to come to be with God in the state of beatitude when they die.

Justification concerns the ways that God moves the individual men so that they can internally accept the Divine grace and virtue for them to be saved in the end. Yet God also gave men objective means to receive the Divine grace and virtue, without which no one can be saved. All of the Divine grace and virtue that comes to men for them to be saved comes from Christ on the Cross. But then Christ and the apostles established the seven sacraments of the Church on earth as the ways for men to internally accept the Divine grace and virtue once God had externally moved them by the Divine grace and virtue. The internal reception of the Divine grace and virtue takes place when men receive the seven sacraments. The seven sacraments of the Church on earth are signs that affect what they signify. Hence a material object or act is a symbol of a deeper spiritual reality. The material sign thus imparts the Divine grace and virtue to the recipient. All of the seven sacraments are human things raised to a higher spiritual level so that men can internally receive the Divine grace and virtue through them. Once the men have internally received the Divine grace and virtue from Christ through the seven sacraments that Christ and the apostles had established for this purpose, they can eventually be saved provided that they die in the possession of the Divine grace and virtue that they received.

But there are also juridical matters to be considered for the seven sacraments. So a proper explanation of these juridical matters is necessary to understand the New Law that Christ established for men to be saved. Once each of the seven sacraments in its juridical context has been considered, it is also necessary to address the nature of the Church on earth as a whole, because the Church on earth is the society of the living who are in the Divine grace and virtue that they had received from Christ through their baptism. Hence it is impossible to consider the Church on earth apart from the seven sacraments in general and baptism in particular as the sacrament that brings men into the Church on earth in the first place. The other matters that concern the nature of the Church on earth as a society will also be addressed in due course once the seven sacraments have been explained in terms of their juridical context.

    The first of the sacraments in the Church on earth, and also one of the two most important of all, is baptism. This is the sacrament by which men first internally receive the Divine grace and virtue from Christ on the Cross in order for them to be saved. This brings men into the Church on earth and makes it possible for them to have recourse to the other sacraments that Christ and the apostles established for men to be saved. When men are baptized into the Church on earth, they bind themselves in their baptism to obey the authorities of the Church on earth as the price of their salvation. Christ established the priesthood of the Church on earth to rule over the rest of the Church in His name and by His authority. More will be said about this when treating Holy Orders. But once men have received the Divine grace and virtue in baptism, they must act in accord with

Christ's will expressed in the doctrine and practices of the Church on earth if they are to preserve the good that they have received. It was said that the Divine grace and virtue in men can be lost after the men have internally received it. Hence there is a need for men to maintain the good received while they live in the fallen world, which takes place by their obedience to what Christ has imposed upon the faithful by the authority that He gave to the priesthood through their ordination to their Order. Christ told the apostles, who were the first priesthood of the Church on earth, that who hears them hears Him as well. This is one of the ways the priests stand in the person of Christ. They do this not only by their ministry to the rest of the faithful, but also the authority that Christ granted to them. So it is necessary for all of the baptized to obey the authorities of the Church on earth. This is the way that they can come to be with God in the state of beatitude.

The significance of baptism among the rest of the sacraments is that it is the first of the sacraments. When the subject receives the Divine grace and virtue from Christ through baptism, this reception establishes a closer relation between Christ and the baptized. The baptized man now knows Christ in a way that he did not before he had entered through baptism into the Church on earth. Since the past cannot be changed, it is impossible for the man to lose this closer relation to Christ that he established when he was baptized into the Church on earth. The closer relation to Christ can deteriorate if the man sins and thus disobeys Christ's will. But it cannot cease to be present with the man. This would mean that the man had never received the initial forgiveness of his sins with the infusion of the Divine grace and virtue. Yet once men have come into the Divine grace and virtue, their former sins cannot return. The sinner lacks a possible good within him because of the sins of which he was guilty, and the Divine grace and virtue that he receives from the sacraments restores him so that he is no longer lacking in the good in the same way that he was before. So the former sins of men, once forgiven, do not return. The man cannot commit the same kinds of sins in the future as he did in the past, with the result that he loses the Divine grace and virtue that he had received from the sacraments. But the same sins as such cannot return to him. As the same sins cannot return in this way, the man cannot lose the closer relation to Christ that he established when he was baptized into the Church on earth. For this reason, baptism can only be received once. There is only one occasion in which a man can receive the Divine grace and virtue for the first time, meaning that any subsequent occasions when the man comes into the

Divine grace and virtue must be done differently. For baptism to ever be repeated would deny that the man had received the Divine grace and virtue in baptism in the first place, which amounts to the sin of unbelief. Hence baptism can only be received once, and other sacraments are needed for the men to return to the Divine grace and virtue that they had initially received in baptism.

      Thus it is evident that baptism is the way that men come into the Church on earth for the first time. Christ told the apostles to make disciples of all nations, baptizing them in the Name of the Trinity. Since Christ acknowledged that men are His disciples when they are baptized, this is how men come into the Church on earth for the first time. But it is also the case that the sacrament of baptism itself takes three different forms. These forms are water, blood, and spirit. St. John the Apostle and Evangelist testified to these when he said that they are all one. This means that men can internally receive the Divine grace and virtue for the first time in three different ways. The Divine grace and virtue received is the same for all men, which means that the men who receive the Divine grace and virtue in any of these ways can be saved if they die with the Divine grace and virtue that God had given to them. Yet while they can all be saved and come to be with God in beatitude, they all necessarily mean that the men baptized in one of these three ways relate differently to the Church on earth.

Baptism by water is the ordinary form of the sacrament, meaning that this is how most of the men receive the sacrament. Most of the men who are saved receive the Divine grace and virtue from Christ because they were washed with water in order to come into the visible and institutional Church on earth. Hence they have dedicated their lives to Christ in order for them to be saved when they die. They are bound in baptism to obey the authorities of the Church on earth for the sake of their own benefit. Baptism by blood means that men who were not baptized with water, but who died as martyrs before they could receive the ordinary form of baptism, are still saved all the same because they were willing to make the ultimate sacrifice of their very lives to Christ for them to be saved. As their death was by a virtuous act, since they were killed by other men for the sake of their faith, it stands to reason that they would go immediately into beatitude with God because they died with the Divine grace and virtue that Christ gave to them at the time of death. This is one of the ways that men can receive the Divine grace and virtue for them to be saved. Baptism by desire means that men who do not know or who do not know properly about the need to be in the visible and institutional Church on earth, but who still live in proper virtue insofar as they know it, can still be saved in the end because they did all that they could for the sake of the good that they understood. Since they failed to enter the visible and institutional Church on earth through no fault of their own, it would be unjust for God to send them to hell on that account. Instead they can come to be with God in the state of beatitude when they die. These are the three forms of the sacrament of baptism by which men can possibly be saved when they die.

Yet baptism by water is still the ordinary means for men to be saved. Baptism by either blood or desire are the two extraordinary means for men to be saved, meaning that they occur far less frequently than baptism by water among the men who are saved when they die. And it cannot be said that baptism by desire is a way that most people or even all people are saved in the end. For men to be baptized in this way means that they must do all that they do for the sake of the greatest possible good as they know it. Given the nature of fallen men, this is difficult for men even with the help that men receive when they are part of the visible and institutional Church on earth. The men who do not have the same help will have much greater difficulty living in proper virtue according to their lesser knowledge. It is far more likely the case that, even if these men lack the faith because God never gave it to them, they will still commit other sins for which they had refused to repent, meaning that they can be sent to hell on that account rather than for their lack of faith. So while it is possible for men to be saved through baptism by desire, this does not mean at all that most men or that all men will be saved in the end. Even taking into account the help that Christ gives for men to be saved, Christ still said that most men are damned in the end. Christ stated that many men are called but few are chosen, and that the road to perdition is wide and the way is easy and that those who find it are many. Christ contrasted this with the way to salvation, which he said is narrow and difficult, and that those who find it are few. Since Christ is God, and God knows all things that can possibly be known, this means that most men are sent to hell when they die. Christ gives His explicit testimony in both of these ways. The exception is that any men are saved at all, given the difficulty that it takes for men to come to God in the end. Christ gives men the help of the Divine grace and virtue from the Cross, but even then most men are still damned. As St. John the Apostle and Evangelist said, the people preferred the darkness to the light.

    Thus it is the nature of baptism that it exists in three different forms. And while the material sign is different for the three different forms, which is how they are distinguished from each other, the Divine grace and virtue conveyed to the recipient is the same in all three cases. The sign differs while the reality is the same. From the way that there are three forms of baptism, it is evident that the number of the elect only partially overlaps with the men who were in the visible and institutional Church on earth. Most of the men who are saved were in the Church on earth when they lived. But there are also many men who were not saved despite being in the Church on earth. And there are some men who are not in the Church on earth in life but who are saved in the end all the same. Christ spoke of the latter when He said that He has other sheep who are not of the same fold. But Christ added that they will be assimilated into the same fold as the rest of His sheep, meaning that they can still come to be with God in beatitude despite the way that they were not in the visible and institutional Church on earth while they were alive.

Since baptism is the first of the seven sacraments, it makes the other sacraments possible to men once they have been received into the Church on earth. Hence baptism is the most necessary of the seven sacraments for men to be saved. Taking into account the three forms of the sacrament of baptism, it can thus be said that God grants salvation to none but the baptized. This means that there is no salvation outside of the Church. Due to the necessity of the sacrament of baptism for men to be saved when they die, it is imperative that men receive baptism as soon as possible after they have been born. It would seem that since infants cannot consent to the reception of the Divine grace and virtue because of their lack of reason, that baptism should be delayed until they are old enough to understand the significance of the sacrament. But this cannot be said. Christ Himself gave precedence to the benefits that children can have from the sacraments when He told the apostles to bring the children to Him for a blessing. The apostles objected that the children could not benefit from coming to Christ because they lacked the full use of their reason, so they could not explicitly understand Who He is. But Christ rebuked them and gave His blessing to the children all the same. Since the children who came to Christ could benefit from Him according to His own testimony, it makes sense that the Church on earth baptizes infants as well. This way they can receive the Divine grace and virtue for them to be saved. Thus in the event that the child dies before he reached the full use of his reason, he can still come to be with God in the state of beatitude. God does not refuse to save the baptized children because they had lacked the use of reason while they were alive.

It may also be said that baptizing children cannot be done without the consent of the parents of the child or those who raise the children as their parents. This pertains to natural law. It was said that the children are a part of their parents in a sense because the bodies of the children come from those of the parents. Hence the parents are entrusted to make the proper decisions for the good of their children until the children become adults. So it would never be acceptable, despite the necessity of baptism for salvation, to take the children from the parents and baptize them without the parental consent. This is contrary to God's will as expressed in the natural law. Since God cannot contradict Himself, God gave the parents their authority over their children, and God also commanded men to be baptized, God's will for men being baptized cannot conflict with His will in giving the parents the dominion over their children. Hence if the parents do not consent to the baptism of their children, the children cannot be baptized. In similar manner it cannot be said that adults can be forcibly baptized into the Church on earth. Adults have the full use of their reason, meaning that for them to receive the reality of the Divine grace and virtue in baptism, they must be open in the free will to receive it. If they are not open in the free will to receive the Divine grace and virtue, no Divine grace and virtue is received.

The mode of reception is in the receiver. And God gave men their free will, meaning that He respects when men resist the reception of the Divine grace and virtue in baptism. Now since God knows all things that can possibly be known, God knows if the man resists in his free will to receive the Divine grace and virtue for him to be saved. Hence other men cannot force a man to receive baptism into the Church on earth. If God does not force His grace and virtue on men for them to be saved, neither can men disregard the free will that God gave to them in order to help the men be saved in the end. A forced baptism is no baptism at all, because the Divine grace and virtue must be freely received if it is to be efficacious for the recipient. At the same time, if a man was compelled to be baptized into the Church on earth in this way, the Church on earth would also suffer at the same time because the man baptized into the Church against his will would not be fully committed to living in accord with the doctrine and practices of the Church on earth. This would mean that he would be a burden in some sense to the rest of the Church on earth because of the sins that he would have committed.

Given the necessity of baptism for men to be saved, the Church on earth has always said that it is possible for anyone to validly baptize someone else provided that actual water is used and the baptism is done using the proper formula, meaning that it is done in the Name of the Trinity. The man who is baptized will then receive the Divine grace and virtue that enables him to be saved when he dies. So while it is proper for the clergy of the Church on earth to baptize men so that the Church on earth as a whole knows who is coming into the Church on earth in order for them to be saved, it is still the case that any man can validly baptize another man if he does so properly and has the intention to baptize the other man. But since the formula for baptism is necessarily said for the recipient to be validly baptized, a man must be baptized by another man. The man cannot baptize himself because then it is impossible for him to say "I baptize you." In this case the man would have to say "I baptize me," which is not the correct formula and would mean that the baptism was not properly ministered to the recipient. So while any man can baptize, it is necessary that the minister and the recipient are different people. If it is not possible for a man to have contact with other men for him to be baptized, this does not have to mean that he will not be saved. The man's own intention to be baptized when it is possible to him would qualify as baptism by desire, meaning that he can still be saved on that account. As it was said, God alone is perfectly just, meaning that God would never hold a man to account for something that is not under his control.

Similarly it cannot be said that many men can baptize one man. This would likewise mean that the formula for the baptism was invalid. If many men were to baptize, the formula would be "we baptize you," which is also incorrect and would mean that the Divine grace and virtue was not ministered to the recipient. The baptism would be invalid in this way as well. It is necessarily the case that the minister who baptizes the recipient uses the singular pronoun because he stands in the person of Christ when he ministers the sacrament. This is the nature of the ministry of the sacraments as such, even in cases when the minister is not an ordained priest. So if a layman or unbeliever baptizes a man into the Church on earth, he would thus stand in the person of Christ when he ministered the sacrament, since all of the Divine grace and virtue of the sacraments comes from Christ. As there is only one Christ, and the minister of the sacrament stands in the person of Christ for the Divine grace and virtue to come to the recipient, it is necessary in baptism that the minister of the sacrament says "I baptize you" rather than "we baptize you." To speak in the plural would make the formula incorrect and the baptism necessarily invalid, meaning that it would have to be done over again properly using the correct formula. It is only when the baptism was properly ministered that the recipient would technically come into the Church on earth in order for him to be saved.

Baptism as the first of the sacraments in the Church on earth is necessarily considered when addressing the laws of the Church on earth, particularly because baptism brings men into the Church on earth for the first time. The Church on earth as a whole is a voluntary society of men who have come together for the sake of their own good so that they can work together in order for them all to be saved when they die. In the same manner as any temporal society, the Church on earth is a perfect thing because she is self-sufficient for the end for which she exists. So while temporal societies are formed by many men coming together to work for their material good, the Church on earth exists for the common spiritual good of her members. Christ and the apostles established the Church on earth so that the faithful can work together for their common benefit. Christ took into account the social nature of men in this way, and He used it for the sake of a higher spiritual good. This is much in the way that the seven sacraments themselves are material signs that affect the spiritual reality that they signify. As the Church on earth is spiritually self-sufficient, she does not need the assistance of any other societies or institutions for her benefit. Yet at the same time, the Church on earth differs from temporal societies because the authority of the Church on earth comes directly from God and not through the agency of other men. Men come together to form their temporal societies so that they give up some of their autonomy to the leaders in the society for their own common good. So while all authority in the created world comes from God, in most cases the authorities that govern men have their power through the agency of other men. This is not the case for the Church on earth. The Church on earth receives her authority directly from Christ, and Christ is both God and man in the one hypostasis. This is important because the men who choose to be bound by the authority of the Christ in the Church on earth consent to be bound in this way through how they were baptized into the Church on earth. This is the price of their salvation, and the way that they can come to be with God in beatitude.

Confirmation is the second of the seven sacraments of the Church on earth. Confirmation gives men an increase in the Divine grace and virtue necessary for them to contend with the greater spiritual threats that come to men when they become adults. The spiritual and the material mirror each other. Just as men are born in the body by one act and grow to become adults by another act, men are born to new spiritual life in baptism and then come into their spiritual adulthood in Confirmation. Now since men take on their spiritual maturity in the Church on earth when they receive this sacrament, it can be said that it gives men an indelible character. Once more the men establish a closer relation to God that did not exist before, and which cannot be taken away once it has been established. As it was said before, this is because the past cannot be changed. Hence the man's future relation to God can deteriorate if the man was to commit sins, but it cannot cease to be the closer relation.

It is evident that Confirmation is a distinct sacrament in the Church on earth from the way that some of the apostles had to go to Samaria for men already baptized to receive the Holy Spirit. The sacrament of Confirmation gives men the protection of the Holy Spirit, just as the apostles had bestowed this upon the baptized. Since the sacrament of Confirmation brings men closer to God and gives the men the increase in the Divine grace and virtue for them to handle the greater spiritual threats of adulthood, this changes the status of the faithful in the Church on earth. They were still members of the Church on earth if they were already baptized, but they are able to participate more fully in the life of the Church on earth once they have obtain to this state of spiritual maturity. While this sacrament is necessary for men to receive in the sense of being needed for them to maintain their grace and virtue, it is not necessary to men in the sense that they need it to be saved in the end. Hence a man who was baptized into the Church on earth but who did not also receive Confirmation can still be saved when he dies provided that he retained the state of the Divine grace and virtue that Christ gave to him when he was baptized into the Church on earth in the first place. Now the sacrament of Confirmation is ordinarily reserved only to the ministry of the bishop. But since bishops and priests are in the same Order, differing from each other only juridically rather than sacramentally, it is possible for a priest who has not been consecrated as a bishop to minister the sacrament of Confirmation to the recipient if the bishop is unavailable. This is also sacramentally valid.

While the Church on earth had initially ministered the sacrament of Confirmation using the laying on of hands, which the apostles did in their time, in subsequent times the sacrament has been ministered with an anointing of oil. Hence the oil itself has become the proper matter for the sacrament, giving men the increase in the Divine grace and virtue as the spiritual reality thereof. That the matter of the sacrament changed from one to the other does not mean that it is either a different sacrament or that something was less rightly done compared to the other ways that the sacrament may be ministered. This is because the Church on earth has a limited authority in some cases to determine the matter and the form that compose the sacrament. A sacrament in general was said to consist of the material sign and the spiritual reality that it signifies. In some cases, as with Confirmation, the material sign is not as strictly determined, meaning that the Church on earth can determine the proper way to minister the spiritual reality to the recipient. It is the same reality received even if the material sign was different. Much of this depends upon the individual case. Hence in the case of the Eucharist, when Christ said to consecrate the bread and wine in remembrance of Him, it is not possible for the matter to be anything other than bread and wine, since this would mean that men did not follow Christ's orders. Yet the case is different for the sacrament of Confirmation, since Christ left it to the apostles to decide how to minister this spiritual reality to the baptized in the Church on earth. Hence the Church on earth, by the same authority that Christ gave to the apostles and which was passed down from them, decided to use an anointing with oil rather than a laying on of hands as the way give men the Divine grace and virtue in the case of this sacrament.

The Eucharist is the most important of the seven sacraments in the Church on earth because it is Christ Himself under the appearance of the bread and wine. Since all of the Divine grace and virtue that comes to men from God comes from Christ on the Cross, this means the Divine grace and virtue of the other sacraments comes from the Eucharist. Christ established the Eucharist as the most important sacrament in the Church on earth so that men can directly unite themselves to Christ on the Cross for the sake of the Divine grace and virtue received. When the faithful receive the Eucharist, they receive the same Christ whole and entire Who offered Himself to God on the Cross. Thus the faithful share in the sacrifice itself that Christ made. And when the Eucharist is consecrated at each Mass, the sacrifice is renewed in order for men to receive Christ. As the very faith of the Church depends upon Christ as the one Who saves men and Who established the Church on earth as the means for men to accept the Divine grace and virtue, it can be said that the Eucharist, as Christ Himself, is at the very center of the faith of the Church on earth.

More can be said about the significance of the Eucharist as the center of the sacramental life of the Church on earth, but much of this is not directly relevant to the juridical aspects of the sacrament itself, which is the subject that is being discussed here. Hence it is necessary to limit the discussion of the Eucharist, as with the other sacraments, to their juridical aspects. Now since the Eucharist is the height of the participation of the faithful in the Church on earth, it is necessarily the case that the faithful can only receive the Eucharist while they are already in the state of the Divine grace and virtue. St. Paul the Apostle made this clear when he said that the men who receive the Eucharist in a state of mortal sin eat and drink judgment onto themselves. Hence it is only proper for the faithful to receive the Eucharist while in a state of the Divine grace and virtue. The spiritual mirrors the material, and the Eucharist is the spiritual food that men receive in order to sustain them in the spiritual life that they had received from Christ in baptism. Hence if men are spiritually dead because of mortal sin, they cannot receive the Eucharist. This is in the same way that ordinary material food would not benefit a dead man. The spiritual food that is the Eucharist cannot benefit men if they are in mortal sin. The men only add to their mortal sin if they receive the Eucharist in sin because they desecrate the sacred species by bringing the species into contact with themselves when they are in a state of mortal sin. At the same time, anyone who ministers the Eucharist to someone known to be in a state of mortal sin becomes an accessory to the mortal sin of the man who unworthily receives the Eucharist. Thus it is of the greatest importance for men that they only receive the Eucharist while in a state of the Divine grace and virtue. If a man already did receive the Eucharist while knowingly in a state of mortal sin, he must go to the sacrament of Penance to confess this along with his other sins so that he can be restored to the Divine grace and virtue through that sacrament.

The purpose of the Eucharist, as the spiritual food that Christ gives to the faithful in the Church on earth, is to sustain the faithful in the Divine grace and virtue that they have already received through the sacrament of baptism. In the same way that material food sustains the body, the spiritual food of the Eucharist sustains men in the soul. Thus if men have suffered from spiritual difficulties while living in the fallen world, or even perhaps if they have diminished the degree of their grace and virtue because they have committed venial sins, they can sustain themselves or restore their higher degree of grace and virtue through receiving the Eucharist. And just as men regularly need material food for them to sustain the body, it is also the case that they can use the Eucharist to spiritually sustain themselves regularly as well. Hence men can receive the Eucharist more than once. Unlike either baptism or

Confirmation, this sacrament does not convey an indelible spiritual character upon the recipient. Since the Eucharist does not convey any spiritual character, it is not strictly necessary for men to receive this sacrament if they are to be saved when they die. Thus if a man was baptized but he did not receive the Eucharist before his death, he would not for that reason be sent to hell when he died. Baptism is the more necessary of the sacraments, and indeed the most necessary of all of the seven sacraments, since it is the only one without which men cannot be saved when they die. Yet at the same time, the Eucharist can still be accorded a particular kind of necessity because it conduces to men being saved. Since the source of the Divine grace and virtue of the other sacraments comes from the Eucharist, it can even be said that the Divine grace and virtue of baptism comes from the Eucharist, meaning that the Eucharist shares in this way in the necessity that is given to baptism for men to be saved when they die.

Given the spiritual benefits that come to the faithful when they receive Christ in the Eucharist, it is proper for the Church on earth to mandate that the faithful receive the Eucharist at least at certain times over the course of the year. It would not be good for the faithful to permanently abstain from receiving the Eucharist. This would mean the faithful refused to participate in their own way in the sacrifice that Christ made of Himself on the Cross and which is renewed in the Mass when the sacred elements are consecrated. Christ told the faithful to commemorate Him in the Eucharist. And all of the faithful must obey this order in their own way in accord with their place in the Church on earth. So while the priests of the Church on earth do this by offering the sacrifice of the Mass for the good of the faithful, the rest of the faithful also commemorate Christ in a different manner when they receive the Eucharist. It must be said that only the role of the priest himself is necessary for Christ to become present under the veil of the consecrated species. It is not necessary for anyone else to do anything or even be present when the Mass occurs. But the faithful can still offer their own participation when they receive the Eucharist. This is even acknowledged in the Mass itself when the priest prays that his sacrifice and that of the others assembled with him will be made acceptable to God. In this case, his sacrifice means the Eucharist that he consecrates during the Mass, while the sacrifice of the rest of the assembled people is themselves whom they offer to God by uniting themselves to Christ through the reception of Christ Himself in the Eucharist. And since the priest alone offers Christ when he consecrates the sacred elements, his sacrifice is the only perfect sacrifice that takes place.

While the sacrifice of the rest of the assembled people with the priest is lesser and imperfect, it is still valuable to God through the way that those who are present choose to unite themselves to Christ in this way for them to be saved.

If it is not possible for the faithful to receive Christ in the Eucharist for the sake of their own benefit, it is still possible for them to make a spiritual communion, where they pray for God to give them the Divine grace and virtue that they would have received from Christ in the ordinary way through the Eucharist. God will still grant the Divine grace and virtue to the recipient in this way provided that he was properly disposed to receive the same. This is because God's will for all things is supremely free, meaning that it is possible for God to grant the effects of the sacrament in some cases without the sign that affects the reality in the way that was already explained. It was said that a sacrament is a material sign that affects the spiritual reality that it signifies. And since God can do all things that are possible, the spiritual reality can be received without the material sign that was ordinarily instituted for that purpose. Hence a man is not strictly prevented by his particular circumstances from receiving the Divine grace and virtue from Christ in the Eucharist. He can make a prayer to God and he will experience the same spiritual effect.

Now since it belongs to the priests of the Church on earth in particular to stand in the person of Christ, the ordained priests of the Church on earth alone have the power to validly consecrate the bread and wine. If the priest is not validly ordained in the Church on earth, or if he does not use the proper formula that Christ instituted and which the Church on earth upholds, then Christ does not become present under the appearance of the bread and wine, meaning that the sacrament is necessarily invalid. It is also likewise invalid if a priest were to try to consecrate something other than bread and wine. Christ told the apostles as the first priesthood of the Church on earth to do what He did at the Last Supper to remember Him. As Christ used actual bread and wine to consecrate for it to become Christ Himself, the Church on earth has no power whatsoever to use other material elements in the Eucharist besides bread and wine. The bread may be either leavened or unleavened as long as it is still actual bread that it used. The Church on earth in different times and places has allowed for either leavened or unleavened bread for the Eucharist. The use of one or the other does not essentially change or invalidate that it is still bread, and that Christ becomes truly present when the words of institution are recited over the bread and the wine for Christ to become present in that place.

The law of the Church on earth requires that the priests only consecrate the Eucharist during the Mass, and that one element cannot be consecrated without the other. This latter concern would mean that the priest did not properly do as Christ did at the Last Supper, since Christ consecrated both of the elements during the same event. It is the case that the bread and wine may have been consecrated at different times over the course of the Passover meal that Christ and the apostles had commemorated, but since it was still the same meal, it constituted one event. So in imitation of Christ, it is not allowed for the priest to consecrate either the bread or the wine without the other element being present. And since the priest who celebrates the Mass in order to consecrate the elements must also receive them, it is the case that the priest must celebrate Mass while he is also in a state of the Divine grace and virtue. The custom of the Church on earth has also said that, absent some compelling circumstances, it is generally only allowed for men to receive the Eucharist once in a day, meaning that priests in general are limited to only celebrating one Mass each day. Yet since this is only the custom, the proper authorities within the Church on earth can dispense with this requirement for the sake of some greater good that may take place.

More can be said about the juridical aspects of the Mass itself, which will be considered when treating the liturgy of the Church on earth as a subject of Church law. Hence it is not necessary here to say more about these matters, since the various laws that concern the celebration of the Mass will be considered in due course.

The sacrament of Penance is the next sacrament that needs to be considered. Penance is necessary as the way for the faithful to be restored to the Divine grace and virtue after they had lost it because they had fallen into mortal sin. Since Penance is for the forgiveness of the sins of the penitent and the restoration to the Divine grace and virtue, it is necessary to consider the different kinds of personal sins that the sacrament can forgive. The sacrament of baptism is the first forgiveness that men receive for their sins. This means that the original sin in particular is forgiven in baptism along with any personal sins at the same time. Thus the recipient receives the Divine grace and virtue along with the indelible character that makes him a member of the Church on earth. Since the sins of men cannot return once they were forgiven, and the original sin is forgiven in baptism, it cannot return. Hence the sacrament of Penance is only for personal sins that men have committed after they were baptized. Since men are not confirmed in either good or evil while they live, they can go back and forth from either one or the other to the converse. So a man in the Divine grace and virtue can either diminish or altogether lose the Divine grace and virtue because of subsequent sins. Why God allows this to happen to men despite receiving the Divine grace and virtue was already explained. The Divine grace and virtue that men receive is not irresistible, meaning that men can commit more sins after baptism that need to be forgiven if the men are to be saved when they die.

Now the personal sins of men, which remain possible to the men after baptism, can be divided as being either mortal or venial sins. Sin in general is to choose a lesser good over the greatest possible good in the given case. Mortal sin means that a man desires a lesser good more than he should, while a venial sin means that a man desires a lesser good more than he should but not more than God. Yet there are some sins that do not admit of any degrees, meaning they are always mortal sins. They can never be venial sins given the context in which they take place. Thus any sexual sins that take place outside of the context of marriage are necessarily mortal sins, since it is only proper for men to engage in any sexual activity within the context of marriage. St. John the Apostle and Evangelist gave the distinction of mortal and venial sins when he said that all sins are evil but that not all sins lead to condemnation. The sins that lead to condemnation are mortal while the other sins are venial.

Since a mortal sin means that a man has desired a lesser good more than God, he makes the lesser good chosen to be the ultimate end for his being. Hence he altogether rejects God. This is how he is said to entirely turn away from God. As the man rejects God fully by the mortal sin, he loses all of the Divine grace and virtue that he had when he committed the sin itself. In juridical terms, this means that he severed himself from the rest of the Church on earth under the rule of Christ. Thus he cannot be admitted to any of the other sacraments unless he is restored to the Divine grace and virtue in union with the rest of the Church. The man does not lose the indelible character that he received from Christ in baptism, but he is no longer actually united to the rest of the Church by the Divine grace and virtue that Christ gives to all of the men in the Church. So if the man wants to be saved when he dies, he must have recourse to the sacrament of Penance to be restored to the Divine grace and virtue that he had lost after baptism.

The case of venial sins is different. A venial sin is when the subject desires a lesser good more than he should but not more than God, which means that he does not essentially reject

God or altogether destroy the Divine grace and virtue that he received. Hence he does not lose his connection to the rest of the Church through the Divine grace and virtue that Christ offers to men. But since the man chose a lesser good in some degree all the same, he diminished the degree of his grace and virtue by what he did, even though he did not altogether destroy it. Since the man did not altogether lose the Divine grace and virtue that Christ gave him, he does not necessarily need the sacrament of Penance to restore the degree of his grace and virtue after a venial sin. God alone can bring being out of non-being because His essence is existence Itself. So God alone can give men the Divine grace and virtue anew when this was lacking to them because of their mortal sins. But since created natures can go from less to more being on their own, men can add to the degree of their grace and virtue after venial sins without having recourse to the sacrament of Penance. Good works add to the degree of a man's grace and virtue. So a man can restore himself to his former degree of grace and virtue after a venial sin simply by doing good works. He does not have to do Penance for his venial sins.

Yet while the man does not necessarily have to go to the sacrament of Penance restore himself to his former degree of grace and virtue, this is always advisable as one of the ways that he might do so. Even if the man had already made up for his venial sins by other good works, it is proper for him to still confess any venial sins in the sacrament of Penance, because this way he can further acknowledge his sinful nature. This means that he can be more open in the free will to receive the Divine grace and virtue that Christ offers to him through the sacrament.

The ordinary minister of the sacrament of Penance is the ordained priest. Since it belongs to the priests of the Church by their Order to stand in the person of Christ, they have the ordinary jurisdiction for the forgiveness of the sins of the penitent man and his restoration to the Divine grace and virtue. God alone can forgive the sins of fallen men, and Christ is both God and man in the one hypostasis, meaning that Christ can forgive the sins of men. Christ forgave the sins of fallen men above all else by His death on the Cross and His rising from the dead. But since the priests of the Church on earth stand in the person of Christ, Christ forgives the sins of men through the acts of the priest to whom the penitent man confesses his sins. And the priest has the ability to decide whether to grant the absolution for the sins to the penitent man or to withhold the same from him in order to move him to a genuine sorrow for the sins that he has committed. Christ told the apostles that whose sins they forgive, they are forgiven them, and whose sins they retain, they are retained, meaning that it is the decision of the priests of the Church on earth, as the successors to the apostles, to decide whether to forgive the sins of the penitent man or to withhold the forgiveness from the man. In the event that the forgiveness is withheld, this is done in order to move the penitent man to a more genuine repentance for the sins that he committed. Once the penitent man has shown that he is truly sorry for the sins that he has committed, he can receive the absolution for them and be readmitted to the spiritual life of the Church on earth.

While the priests of the Church on earth are the ordinary ministers of the sacrament of Penance, it is possible for men to validly confess their sins either directly to God or even to a layman in order to receive absolution. This has been done in certain times in the history of the Church on earth, and this practice was recognized as a valid way for men to receive the Divine grace and virtue that they need for the forgiveness of their sins. Thus if a man confesses his sins either directly to God or to a layman who grants him the absolution, the man can be saved when he dies in the same way as if he had confessed to a priest. This is possible because the Divine will for all things is supremely free, meaning that God is not strictly limited to the material signs of the seven sacraments to grant the Divine grace and virtue to men for them to be saved. Yet if a man receives the Divine grace and virtue of the sacrament of Penance in one of these other ways, he must still confess to a priest in the Church afterwards so that he can be readmitted to the other sacraments. But if this does not occur, and the man dies before he gets to confess to a priest, he would still go to heaven when he died. He would not f be sent to hell because he still received the Divine grace and virtue from Christ when he confessed either to God or to a layman in anticipation of going to a priest of the Church on earth.

This is the nature of the minister of the sacrament itself and how he relates to the penitent man as the recipient thereof. Now it necessary to consider the three parts of the sacrament itself. The three parts of the sacrament of Penance are contrition, confession, and satisfaction. First the penitent man is sorry for the sins that he had committed by which he had offended God. Then he confesses the sins themselves to the minister of the sacrament. Finally he makes up for the sins that he committed by doing some good work to restore the former degree of his grace and virtue. From the juridical perspective, the man is fully restored to the fold of the Church on earth when he receives the absolution after he had confessed his sins. This means that the man is back in the

Divine grace and virtue. God has restored the man to the Divine grace and virtue through the acts of the minister of the sacrament, meaning that if the man was to die at that time, he could still eventually be saved. But while the absolution brings the man back to the fold of the Church on earth and makes it possible for the man to be saved in the end, the man still has to make satisfaction for his sins. The sins that the man had committed damaged the contrary good habit that the man had within himself before he committed the sin. If the sin was mortal, the Divine grace and virtue was altogether destroyed in the man while the good habit was weakened at the same time. Then once the man is restored to the Divine grace and virtue, he receives the Divine grace and virtue to a lesser degree than he had it before he had sinned. This is because of the way that the sin that he had committed damaged the contrary good habit. So to build back the good habit after the man damaged the habit through his sin, he has to do some good work. This can bring the new Divine grace and virtue that God gave him back to the former degree so that it is as if the man had not sinned at all. Thus if the man dies once he has made satisfaction after the absolution, he has all of the Divine grace and virtue that was possible to him, meaning that he can be saved immediately. If he did not make satisfaction before he died, he will have to go to purgatory before he can come to be with God in beatitude.

Purgatory is where men are sent if they were in venial sin. It was said that mortal sin totally destroys the Divine grace and virtue that the man had received from God. Since the mortal sinner altogether lacks the Divine grace and virtue, if he dies without it, he is confirmed in his evil and sent to hell when he dies. But venial sins damage the degree of the Divine grace and virtue in the man without altogether destroying the Divine grace and virtue in the manner of mortal sin. This means that man has less of the Divine grace and virtue than is possible to him at the time, although he still possesses the Divine grace and virtue in some degree. Now if a man dies while he lacks some of the Divine grace and virtue, he still owes it to God to make up for the way that he is lacking some of the Divine grace and virtue that was possible to him. So God sends the men to purgatory for them to make up to God by their suffering there for the way that they lacked some of the Divine grace and virtue that was possible to them in life. It is only when they have paid back to God for their lack of the Divine grace and virtue that they can come to be with God in the state of beatitude. And since the man who died without making satisfaction still owes some good to God as well, it is possible for him to be sent to purgatory to make up for the sins of which he had been absolved but for which he still had to make some satisfaction. Yet if the man had died while still intending to make the satisfaction for the sins that he had committed which had already been absolved, God would not reasonably hold this against the man. This would be to punish the man in purgatory for his diminished grace and virtue when he did not have the possibility in life to avoid the punishment. So the man in this case would still reasonably be sent to heaven when he dies because it would be unjust for him to go to purgatory in this case, and God alone is perfectly just. For which reason these are the three parts of the sacrament of Penance itself, as well as the different effects that they have on men in life.

Since it is the nature of venial sins that they only diminish rather than destroy the Divine grace and virtue in the subject, it can be said that men can use their own good works without going to the sacrament of Penance to restore themselves after the sins that they had committed. This is because while God alone can bring being out of non-being, and thus forgive the mortal sins of men, different created natures can make more being where there was less being, meaning that men can add to the degree of their Divine grace and virtue in order to restore it after they had committed venial sins. Thus a man can substitute a good work of some kind for the satisfaction that he would make after his sins were absolved in the sacrament of Penance. Since one good work can add to the degree of the man's grace and virtue in the same way as any other, a man does not have to make satisfaction for his sins if he does other good works. These are the indulgences that are possible to men while they are alive. If a man performs an indulgence, he can make up for the former venial sins on his own without having recourse to the sacrament of Penance. The man can also use an indulgence to make up for mortal sins once he has already gone to the sacrament of Penance and been restored through absolution to the Divine grace and virtue. What ultimately matters is that the man does the good work rather than that the particular good work done is meant to counter the loss of the degree of the Divine grace and virtue because of his venial sins. The man is still restored one way or the other to the fullest degree of the Divine grace and virtue possible to him if he had not sinned in the first place. And if the man uses the indulgence in place of the satisfaction, this also means that he can avoid having to make up for those sins if he was sent to purgatory. Thus the man in this case is still restored to the fold of the Church on earth, and he can be admitted to the other sacraments.

Extreme Unction is the other sacrament in the Church on earth that can be used many times to restore men to the Divine grace and virtue. This one differs from the sacrament of Penance because it prepares the subject to die in the Divine grace and virtue so that he can go to heaven when he dies. Hence this sacrament is only ministered to men who are sick and in danger of death. It is evident that the apostles had established this as one of the seven sacraments of the Church on earth. St. James states that if anyone in the Church is sick that the priests of the Church should pray over him so that he can receive the Divine grace and virtue in preparation for death. It is also possible that God may even grant miraculous healing to the man who has received the sacrament, although this is rare and is not an essential part of the sacrament itself. It is also not the intention thereof, since the intention of the sacrament is for men to receive the Divine grace and virtue in the event that he dies. Like the sacrament of Penance, it is possible for a man to receive this sacrament more than once. Neither of these two sacraments imparts an indelible character on the recipient, meaning that they can be received as many times as it appears necessary. Thus a man should receive the sacrament of Penance any time that he has committed at least a mortal sin if not also a venial sin, and a man can receive Extreme Unction as many times as the man may be in danger of death. This way the man can be prepared for the particular judgment that God gives to men at the time of death. And it is the case that the proper minister of this sacrament is the ordained priest because the priest as such stands in the person of Christ by his authority to minister to the faithful for them receive the Divine grace and virtue. This way the men can be saved. And since men receive the particular judgment at the time of death, it makes sense that the Church on earth would institute a sacrament to particularly help men at the time of death so that they have a better possibility to receive a favorable judgment from God when they die.

Holy Orders is the sacrament that allows the Church on earth to continue to minister to the faithful so that they can receive the Divine grace and virtue. Christ gave His assurance to the Church on earth that she would continue from the time of the First Coming to the time of the Second Coming. For the Church on earth to continue Christ's ministry for fallen men to be saved, it is necessarily the case that there is Holy Orders in the Church on earth. This way the men who have been ordained to the priesthood in particular can devote themselves to serving the faithful by the way that they stand in the person of Christ to give men the Divine grace and virtue from the seven sacraments. And it is by the seven sacraments of the Church on earth that the faithful can unite themselves to Christ on the Cross for them to be saved when they die.

Now it is evident that Christ Himself had ordained the apostles as the first priesthood in the Church on earth. Christ took the apostles to a high mountain, laid hands on them and prayed over them, and then sent them out with the proper instructions so that they could bring the Gospel to men. Then the apostles instituted the diaconate in the Church on earth so that there were other men charged with managing the material affairs of the Church on earth while the apostles, as the priesthood of the Church on earth, were busy ministering to men, preaching to them, and praying to God. These are the two Orders that have been in the Church on earth since the time of the apostles. At later times the Church on earth has instituted other Orders to which men were also ordained. But since these other Orders were neither of Divine or apostolic origin, they were not sacred Orders in the manner of the priesthood or the diaconate. It can also be said that the episcopacy developed out of the priesthood as well. In the earliest times in the Church on earth, there was only the priests and the deacons. But as the Church on earth grew over time, it became necessary for there to be a juridical distinction within the priesthood so that some priests were set over others. Hence the priests who exercise the fullness of the Order are the bishops, since they have the authority and the ability to minister all seven sacraments. The other priests in the Church on earth still have the ability, but they do not have the authority, since this is restricted to the bishops alone. Hence it can be said that the episcopacy is the fullness of the Order of the priesthood. But that the episcopacy is not an Order in itself is evident from how the priests and deacons of the Church on earth are ordained while the bishops are consecrated. It is a juridical difference that exists between the bishops and the other priests of the Church on earth rather than the character of a distinct Order. This is according to the custom of the Church on earth rather than any Divine or apostolic institution.

    Yet the priesthood and the diaconate, as the two Orders of the Church on earth, both establish an indelible character in the soul of the recipient. Since this is an indelible character imparted to the recipient, it can only be received once. Once the man is ordained in particular as a priest of the Church on earth, he remains as a priest for the rest of his life. Thus the priests of the Church receive the ability to stand in the person of Christ to minister to the faithful. And Christ Himself instituted the priesthood as the way for the Church on earth to continue until the Second Coming. Christ also gave the priests of the Church on earth their essential authority over the rest of the faithful in the Church on earth. Since it is the priests of the Church on earth who stand in the person of Christ, and Christ rules over all things because He is both God and man in the one hypostasis, it thus makes sense that the priests who stand in His place on earth would also exercise their own authority over the rest of the Church on earth. Thus Christ gave the apostles as the first priests of the Church on earth the power of the keys. Christ told them that what they bind or loose on earth shall be bound or loosed in heaven. This means that they have the final authority under God in the Church on earth, and that God will support the decisions that they choose to make for the good of the faithful. Yet so that this authority that Christ gave to the apostles and to the priesthood is not abused, Christ sent the Holy Spirit into the Church on earth to protect the Church on earth from all error in her sacred doctrine and practices. This means that the Church on earth will retain all of her essential characteristics from the time of the First Coming to the time of the Second Coming. This is called the indefectibility of the Church on earth, about which more will later be said.

Given that there is the juridical distinction between the episcopacy and the rest of the priesthood, it makes sense that only the bishops would be legally allowed to ordain men to Holy Orders. It would be possible for a priest who has not been consecrated as a bishop to do the same, but while he possesses the ability to do so as a priest, he does not have the authority. And it is necessarily the case that someone who has not been ordained to Holy Orders necessarily lacks the ability to ordain someone else. What one does not possess in the first place, one cannot give to others. Hence a man who lacks the indelible character of the priesthood cannot ordain someone else to the priesthood. It likewise makes sense that no one can be ordained to the diaconate except by a priest. Since the lower is contained in the higher, it is possible for a priest as someone in the Order above the diaconate to legitimately ordain a deacon to his Order in the Church on earth. At the same time, it is not possible for a deacon to ordain anyone in the Church on earth, even to the diaconate, since it is the priest, who by standing in the person of Christ, has the power to impart the character of the Order to the man who is thus ordained.

It must be said that it is never possible for any woman to be ordained to Holy Orders in any degree. The priests of the Church on earth stand in the person of Christ to minister to the faithful. Hence the priests of the Church on earth are married to the Church, as the Church is considered to be the spouse of Christ Himself. So if the Church on earth is understood as female, the priests of the Church on earth have to be male. It is not possible under any circumstance for a woman to receive the indelible character of either the priesthood or the diaconate. Even if the rite of ordination was to be performed on a woman, she would not receive the indelible character of the Order proper to the rite itself. The man who is ordained to Holy Orders is the matter of the sacrament while the prayers said over him are the form. The matter and the form together compose the sacrament. If one or the other is not present, then the effect of the sacrament does not take place. This means that no indelible character is conferred on the recipient. And the proper matter for Holy Orders is the man to be ordained. It has been supposed that there was a time when women were at least ordained to the diaconate, but this was never actually the case. There was a time when women were given the duty of baptizing other women back when adult baptism was more common and the one baptized was nude when in the water. The Church did not believe that it was becoming for a man to baptize nude women, so this task was given to other women in the Church. But this is not a major concern for the understanding of Holy Orders in the Church on earth, because these women were never thought to be ordained. And it was already said that anyone can validly baptize because of the necessity of baptism for men to be saved. So it was not a problem that women rather than men ministered the baptism to other women, since it is still possible to this day for anyone, male or female, to minister a valid baptism to the recipient. Hence men alone can be ordained to Holy Orders, meaning that it is impossible for any woman to ever receive this sacrament in any degree whatsoever.

More can be said concerning the authority of those in Holy Orders over the rest of the Church on earth or the different offices in the Church hierarchy held by ordained clergy. These will be treated concerning the matters of Church authority in general, as well as the duties and obligations of the faithful to the Church on earth as a whole for the good of their souls. Such things are indeed necessary for men to be saved when they die, meaning it is proper to consider them in their place. It is also highly relevant to the juridical nature of the Church on earth as an institution endowed with the ability to make laws that are to be obeyed by the faithful for their salvation.

Matrimony is the least of the seven sacraments within the Church on earth because it was instituted only as an acceptable way for men and women to engage in sex and to raise the children they conceived together in the sexual act. Christ and the apostles both made it clear that it is better for men and women alike to retain their virginity. This way they can be directly devoted to God instead of only being indirectly devoted to God through the spouse. Hence Christ said that those who can retain their virginity by going for their entire lives without sex ought to do this for their own good, and the apostles concurred with this belief when Christ asked them. St. Paul the Apostle further elaborated on how it is not expedient for men and women to get married because of the way that a spouse and children would be distracting from God. Yet St. Paul still concluded that it is better for men to be married than to burn in hell because they could not sexually control themselves and committed the sin of fornication. And St. Paul described matrimony as a sacrament of the Church on earth. While matrimony has always existed within human society, Christ and the apostles chose to elevate it to a higher level so that the men and women in the marriage can receive the Divine grace and virtue from their union. The sacraments are material things that were elevated to the level of spiritual significance so that the recipient could obtain the Divine grace and virtue. So baptism is a washing, the Eucharist is a meal, and so forth. These are ordinary material things that have been elevated to a higher state so that men can receive the Divine grace and virtue from them. And St. Paul explained the sacramental nature of marriage when he said that a man loves his wife in the way that Christ loves the Church on earth. This influences the Church's understanding of marriage as one of the seven sacraments instituted by Christ and the apostles for the good of the faithful.

Now this does not mean that marriages that have not been contracted in the Church on earth are not valid unions. They are valid as natural unions but not as sacraments. For a marriage to be sacramental, and thus recognized in the Church on earth, it must be contracted with the intention of both parties so that they intend to receive the Divine grace and virtue through their union. The intention of the recipient determines if the Divine grace and virtue is actually received, meaning that if the couple did not intend to be bound in the Church by a sacramental marriage, no Divine grace can be received and the union would not be recognized by the Church on earth. While such a marriage might be an occasion for virtue for the spouses, this does not mean that they received any Divine grace and virtue from the union at the same time.

Like all of the other sacraments in the Church on earth, matrimony has both matter and form. The matter of the sacrament is the couple whose union symbolizes that of Christ with the Church, and the form of the sacrament is the vows that the husband and wife recite to each other. And just as Christ is always faithful to the Church on earth, the husband and the wife are bound to each other for the rest of their natural lives. Christ Himself attested to the same when He said that it is not possible for a man and woman to divorce. The marriage that was formed is a contract where both of the spouses agree to have the exclusive use over the other one's body for the purposes of sex. And it is within the vows that they will be faithful to each other until death, despite any different negative consequences that can happen to them while they are together. So the vows are the terms of the contract. Since the vows explicitly say that the spouses will be faithful to each other for the rest of their natural lives, for them to try to divorce would be to try to break up a union, that according to its terms, can only end in the death of one or both of the spouses. Hence any attempt of the spouses to divorce each other is necessarily invalid and cannot be recognized by the Church on earth.

While a valid marriage cannot be dissolved by a divorce, it is still the case that some unions between a man and a woman do not work out for the better of the two of them. It becomes evident over time that the union was not the occasion for either one of them adding to the Divine grace and virtue that they had intended to receive when they were first married. In which case it is entirely possible that the union itself was invalid from the very beginning. Christ attested to how this is possible when He spoke to the woman at the well. Christ asked her if she was married and she replied that she was not. Christ told her that she spoke correctly, since she had been married four times. Hence it is evident that a validly contracted marriage might not be valid in the first place. So while marriage lasts until the death of one or both of the spouses, it is still possible that a marriage that comes to an end was never a valid marriage in the first place, either as a union or as a sacrament. Since the Church on earth, by the power of binding and loosing, has the authority to determine the validity of a sacrament, the Church on earth can annul a marriage in the event that it did not become a means for the spouses to receive the Divine grace and virtue. But given the serious nature of what takes place, the Church on earth must use the greatest discretion when deciding to annul a marriage. For this reason, the Church on earth has decided according to her juridical authority that all marriages that have been validly contracted between a man and a woman are assumed to be valid as marriages and as sacraments unless there is some compelling reason for them to decide otherwise. This works to better preserve the integrity of matrimony, both as a union and a sacrament of the Church on earth. The Church on earth does have the proper authority to annul a marriage, but this must always be done with the greatest discretion.

There is also the matter of who can form a valid marriage in the first place. The natural limits that exist according to the definition of marriage have already been considered. Thus any union that necessarily lacks the procreative aspect cannot be called a marriage under any circumstances. But there are other ways that it is not proper to form a marriage. The first way is if the marriage is formed between two blood relatives, which is prohibited from happening because then the offspring conceived and born in the union would be defective. For the good of the children's health, it is not possible to form a valid marriage between two blood relatives. However, since the Church on earth has the authority to regulate the ways that marriages are contracted in the first place, the Church on earth can determine what degree of blood relation is prohibited from forming the marriage contract. And the Church at different times throughout her history has modified the degrees of kinship that are prevented from contracting a valid marriage. In some cases the Church on earth has decided to follow the civil authorities where this is reasonable, but this does not change that it remains within the discretion of the Church authorities to make this decision all the same. The second relation that is prevented from forming a valid marriage is legal relations, meaning that a man or a woman cannot marry any in-laws. This is the relationship of affinity. Since legal relations follow the natural relations, it is not possible for someone to marry any in-laws if the former spouse dies. The third kind of prohibited relation is godparents with their godchildren. Now the spiritual mirrors the material, meaning that just as the bodily parents of the children are necessarily prohibited from marrying their own offspring, the same is the case for godparents and godchildren. Hence the three kinds of prohibited relationships are blood relatives, legal relatives, and spiritual relatives. Any such relations would not work for the greater good which is the proper end of the marriage contract, meaning that such unions must be dissolved if they were to be contracted. In the event that someone marries within one of these categories but was unaware of the relation at the time, no sin is incurred, but the marriage must still be dissolved because it is necessarily illegitimate.

Since Christ said that the marriage is to last for the entire time that the spouses are alive, it is the case that the material goods that the husband and wife had acquired in the marriage are passed down to their children. This is one of the ways that the children can benefit from the marriage even when they are in adulthood. In the event that there are any illegitimate children from one or both of the spouses, any legitimate children are given the priority over the inheritance because they were the natural products of the marriage. Only then can the illegitimate children receive some of the material goods once the spouses have died. Aside from the inheritance, it is proper that the illegitimate children be treated the same as the legitimate children. It is never just to hold someone to account for what he did not do of his own accord, meaning that since the illegitimate children did not choose to be born under such a condition, they should not be treated any less than anyone else because this would necessarily be unjust. They should be part of the same family as the other children.

These are the different juridical aspects of all of the seven sacraments in the Church on earth. It is evident from this the ways that Christ and the apostles established the seven sacraments in the Church on earth as the means for men to receive the Divine grace and virtue of Christ on the Cross. Since baptism as the first of the seven sacraments brings men into the Church on earth for the first time, the nature of baptism is essential to the Church on earth as a legal institution. The Church on earth is the society of all of the baptized who are united to Christ and to each other by the way that they received the Divine grace and virtue from Christ in the sacrament of baptism. The other sacraments of the Church on earth likewise determine how the individual men in the Church on earth relate to the rest of the Church on earth and to Christ above all else as the supreme head of the whole Church. Thus the sacrament of Penance brings men back into the fullness of the fold of the Church on earth because it restores men to the Divine grace and virtue once this was lacking to them because of sins committed after baptism. Any mortal sins committed after baptism separate the subject from the rest of the Church on earth, since the faithful in the Church are united to God and to each other by the Divine grace and virtue. So Penance restores the men to their proper condition within the Church on earth. And the sacraments of Holy Orders and matrimony both establish particular roles in the Church on earth for the men who receive them. The men who enter into these states can offer some particular good to the Church on earth for the perfection of the Church on earth as a Divine society.

Having addressed the juridical matters concerning the seven sacraments, it remains to address the juridical aspects of the Church on earth as a whole. It was said that the Church on earth is a spiritual society. The spiritual mirrors the temporal, meaning that just as men form temporal societies for the sake of their own material good, they similarly come together in the Church on earth for the sake of their higher spiritual good. But while the individual men in the temporal society come together to form the temporal state that rules over them, Christ Himself gave the Church on earth her essential characteristics when He established the Church on earth at the time of the First Coming. Hence the authority of the Church on earth comes directly from Christ as both God and man, and it does not depend upon the consent of the individual men who are in the Church on earth. This is the most important difference from the Church on earth as the one spiritual society of Christ and the temporal states that men form for the sake of their material good. Yet just as the temporal society is governed by a temporal state, the Church as the spiritual society is also governed by rulers as well. Christ and the apostles established the Church on earth to be who she is, meaning that she can never depart from these essential characteristics that she had received from them. That the Church on earth lacks the ability to depart from her essential characteristics is the indefectibility of the Church on earth. The indefectibility means two things. First, it means that the Church on earth that Christ had established at the time of the First Coming will endure until the time of the Second Coming. Second, it means that the Church on earth will always preserve her essential characteristics for that entire time. Hence the Church on earth cannot suffer destruction in the fallen world and she cannot cease to be the Church on earth as she was established by Christ and the apostles.

Now Christ Himself guaranteed the indefectibility of the Church on earth when He taught men about the Church at the First Coming. First, Christ said that the gates of hell would not prevail against the Church on earth, meaning that she would survive until the time of the Second Coming and that she would not cease to be the institution that Christ and the apostles had established for men to be saved. Second, Christ prayed that the faith of the Church on earth would not fail. Since Christ is God and man in the one hypostasis, Christ knows all things that can possibly be known. So Christ knows which prayers to make so that the prayers will ultimately be fulfilled in the end. Thus any prayers that Christ makes are necessarily always fulfilled. Hence when Christ prayed that the faith of the Church on earth would not fail, this means that the Church on earth will always be who she is and that she will endure until the time of the Second Coming. Third, Christ said that heaven and earth will pass away but His words will not pass away. The doctrines of Christ are contained in their perfection in the Church on earth. Hence if Christ's words will not pass away, this means that the Church on earth will endure until the time of the Second Coming, and that she will not cease to be the Church on earth throughout that time. This means that the Church on earth cannot defect. Fourth, Christ told the faithful in the Church on earth that He would send them the Holy Spirit, and this took place on Pentecost. So the Holy Spirit remains in the Church on earth and guides the Church on earth so that she can never lose any of her essential characteristics in terms of her doctrine and practices. Since the Holy Spirit thus protects the Church on earth, the Holy Spirit is God, and God does all things perfectly, it must be said that the Church on earth cannot defect because of the Holy Spirit. Fifth, Christ told the faithful in the Church on earth that He would be with them always, even to the consummation of the world. This means that Christ will not cease to be with the Church on earth. As Christ is with the Church on earth in this way, He will protect the Church on earth so that she cannot defect. Sixth, Christ said that He would not leave the faithful as orphans. This would indeed have happened if it was possible for the Church on earth to be destroyed or to be changed into something other than what God had intended the Church on earth to be. This means that Christ thus gave His assurance that the Church on earth cannot defect. These are all of the different ways that it can be said that the Church on earth possesses the quality of being indefectible. This is grounded in the words of Christ Himself, Who is both God and man in the one hypostasis, and Who knows all things that can be known because He is both God and man. Hence if Christ knows the future, when He said that the Church on earth is indefectible, this must necessarily be the case. This is the ultimate meaning of all of the different statements that Christ made that have been considered.

While it is impossible for the Church on earth to ever defect in terms of her most essential characteristics, this does not mean that it is not possible for the Church on earth to suffer from corruption in certain times and places. Christ also said that this would indeed happen when He told men the parable of the wheat and the cockle growing together in the field. Christ said on that occasion that the kingdom of heaven was the field, the Father was the farmer, the devil was the enemy, the virtuous men in the Church were the wheat, the evil men in the Church were the cockle, the harvesters were the angels, the barn was heaven, and the fire was hell. The farmer told the harvesters that they should wait until the harvest to gather what grew in the field. Only then would the wheat and the cockle be separated from each other. The farmer said to proceed this way so that the wheat would not be damaged if the cockle was harvested before the regular time. Both the wheat and the cockle would be taken to different places, meaning the virtuous men would go to heaven and the wicked would be sent to hell. Christ told the faithful here, as He explained it more clearly to the apostles, that the Church on earth whom He founded for men to be saved would suffer from corruption. But this does not take away from the legitimate authority of the Church on earth or that she is the Church on earth that Christ founded.

Christ did not directly refer to the Church as such when He told this parable to the people, but it is evident that the kingdom of heaven, as He called it, is the Church on earth. If the cockle represents the evil men, this cannot possibly be heaven itself, because there would be no evil men in heaven. And Christ also said that the cockle, as the evil men, would be thrown on the fire, where the fire is taken to represent the fire of hell that punishes the evil for their unrepented sins. Hence it is clear that the barn that was mentioned in the parable is heaven and the fire is hell, where the field as the kingdom of heaven is the Church on earth. This also accords with how the Church on earth is understood as the beginning of the kingdom of heaven on earth. The Church on earth is the way for men to be saved, so that there is no salvation outside of the Church on earth. Since the men in the Church on earth who are saved in the end will also come to live with Christ and the angels in the New Heaven and New Earth, it can thus be said that the Church on earth between the First Coming and the Second Coming is the beginning of the New Heaven and New Earth. Now the New Heaven and New Earth is the kingdom of God in its fullness, meaning that the Church on earth before that time is the beginning of the kingdom of God on earth. This is likewise apparent from other times when Christ mentioned the kingdom of God that He thus refers to the Church on earth that He established. Christ told the faithful that the kingdom of God was at hand, meaning that He had come to earth at that time to establish the Church on earth. And since men must be in the Church on earth in order for them to be saved when they die, the men who seek salvation from Christ must be baptized into the Church on earth whom He founded for that very purpose.

There are many essential characteristics that belong to the Church on earth. Among these characteristics are the seven sacraments that Christ and the apostles established, which have already been considered in terms of their juridical nature. But there are other characteristics as well. Since Christ placed primacy on the need to be in the Church on earth that He founded in order for men to be saved, it is necessarily the case that the Church on earth is a visible institution. This way men can know the location of the Church on earth for them to be one of the members thereof. Christ said that if men love Him, they will obey His precepts. And one of the precepts that Christ gave to the Church on earth was the Great Commission. Christ told the faithful to baptize all nations in the Name of the Trinity so that as many men as possible can come into the Church on earth in order for them to be saved. Hence it is incumbent upon the faithful in this way to be baptized into the Church on earth for them to receive from Christ on the Cross the Divine grace and virtue that allows them to be saved when they die. For men to fulfill this precept that Christ gave to men, men must know where they can find the true Church in order for them to be baptized into the Church so that they can possibly be saved when they die.

Hence it cannot be said that the Church on earth is an invisible society of men united to Christ without knowing it. While men in life cannot say for sure if they will be saved because they do not know the future, men do need to know what is required of them for them to be saved. Since men must be in the Church on earth to be saved, it is necessary that the Church is a visible institution in order for men to know how to become part of the Church. Otherwise it would be impossible for men to fulfill this precept. God gives men His precepts for them to observe them, since it would make no sense for God to impose a rule on men that could never possibly be fulfilled. This would be to no purpose, and God does nothing without purpose. So it is necessarily one of the characteristics of the Church on earth that she is a visible institution.

Another essential characteristic of the Church on earth that she is a perfect society. This can be said in three different ways. First, this means that the Church on earth is spiritually self-sufficient, so that she needs nothing from any other sources for the men in the Church on earth to be saved when they die. It is the purpose of the Church on earth to save souls, so that the highest law in the Church on earth is the salvation of souls. If Christ Who founded the Church on earth was to establish a society that was not spiritually self-sufficient, it would mean Christ did something that was less than perfect. But God is perfect and Christ is both God and man in the one hypostasis, meaning that all that comes from God and Christ must be perfect in its own way as well. This is because the effect always resembles the cause in order for it to be the effect of that cause. So if God and Christ do all things perfectly, the Church on earth that Christ had founded for men to be saved must have all that men need if they are indeed to be saved when they die. This is one of the ways that the Church on earth is a perfect society. It can similarly be said that temporal societies are perfect in their own way as well, since the temporal society does not need anything from outside in the way that this can be said for individual men. Individual men cannot survive on their own in the way that this is possible to a society of men. So a temporal society is perfect relative to the material goods that are the proper end thereof. And the Church on earth, as a society, is perfect concerning the spiritual ends to which she is directed for the salvation of her members.

Second, the Church on earth is a perfect society in the sense that there is no further public revelation from God that men need to know beyond what Christ revealed at the First Coming and which the Church on earth has preserved as her sacred doctrine. Christ Himself said from the

Cross that the public revelation was finished at the time of the First Coming. Hence the public revelation that God gave to mankind ended with the death of the last of the apostles. Now this does not mean that individual men in the Church on earth cannot still receive private revelations beyond what is contained in the public revelation. But it is the nature of all private revelations as such that they are not binding on anyone but the men who immediately receive them. And the purpose of the private revelations that God gives to men is to bring men back to the public revelation that Christ and the apostles had completed at the time of the First Coming. So there is no further public revelation that can take place after Christ. It is also proper that Christ would be the end of the public revelation because all of the Divine revelations ultimately concern God, and Christ is both God and man in the one hypostasis. So when God became man as Christ, it is necessarily the case that nothing beyond Christ is needed for men to be saved. Christ and the apostles gave men the final Divine revelation that men need if they are to come to be with God in the state of beatitude when they die.

Third, the Church on earth is a perfect society in the sense that the Holy Spirit guides the Church on earth so that she is necessarily free from all error in terms of her sacred doctrine and practices. This was already treated earlier concerning the indefectibility of the Church on earth. Hence when the Church on earth, guided by the Holy Spirit, officially declares a doctrine in matters of faith and morals to be held by all of the faithful, this doctrine must necessarily be true. While the public revelation of God to mankind ended with the death of the last of the apostles, it is still proper for the Church on earth at different times in her history to define certain doctrines and to require the faithful to give their assent to them for the sake of their own spiritual good. This way the men can better understand the nature of God through the Divine revelation, which means that they can love God more if they know Him better in this way. By that love, they can come closer to God in the hope of being with God in the state of beatitude. The authority of the Church on earth to make such declarations comes from Christ Who gave the apostles as the first priesthood of the Church on earth the power of binding and loosing. So when the authorities in the Church on earth declare that certain doctrines are to be held by all of the faithful, the faithful must comply for the sake of their own spiritual good. And the faithful can be sure that such declarations are free from all error because the Holy Spirit guides the Church on earth to protect her from all error.

The authority of the Church on earth to make declarations on matters of faith and morals that are binding on all of the faithful concerns the Church's possession of infallibility. The Holy Spirit guides the Church on earth in order to protect her from all error in terms of her sacred doctrine and practices. As the Holy Spirit is God, and God alone is infallible, it is necessarily the case that the Church on earth also possesses the ability to infallibly declare doctrines that are binding on all of the faithful in the Church on earth for the sake of their own spiritual good. Thus the faithful can better know and love God, which is how this is done for the salvation of their souls. Now most of the infallible declarations in the Church on earth have been made by ecumenical councils. Hence when an ecumenical council intends to make a formal declaration on matters of faith and morals, and such a declaration is actually made, it is binding on all of the faithful on pain of sin to give their assent to it. This means that they are bound to believe for their own spiritual benefit what the Church on earth had infallibly proclaimed. Yet while most of the infallible declarations in the history of the Church have been made by ecumenical councils, it is also possible for the pope, as the highest authority under God in the Church on earth, to make an infallible declaration without the help of an ecumenical council. The pope and not an ecumenical council is the highest authority under God within the Church on earth, meaning that the decisions of any ecumenical councils are only legitimate if they have been endorsed by the reigning pope. Since the pope is the supreme power over the Church on earth under God, the pope can also make such a declaration on his own as well. The authority of any declarations of papal infallibility carry the same weight as declarations that were made by an ecumenical council. They are no less binding on the faithful for that reason, meaning that the faithful are still obligated on pain of sin to give the assent of their belief to what was infallibly declared.

Now the infallibility of the declarations of the Church on earth can be considered as being of one of three different categories. The first category for infallible statement is ordinary infallibility, which means that the statement itself that was made was already officially recognized as one of the immutable doctrines of the Church on earth at a previous time. Hence it is possible that the Church on earth or one of the authorities in the Church will state something that reflects what the Church has already believed as having been inspired by God. This is the meaning of ordinary infallibility. Technically it is possible for anyone in the Church on earth to make such a statement because the doctrines in this case have already been defined. Hence if someone in the Church is to affirm with the theological faith that God gives that God Himself is one God in three persons or three persons in one God, thus referring to the Trinity, this is an statement of ordinary infallibility. This statement accords with what the Church on earth has already infallibly defined as an immutable doctrine of the faith that is binding on all of the faithful to give their assent on pain of sin. The second category of infallible statements is extraordinary infallibility, which refers to statements made by the authorities in the Church on earth with the intention of making the particular doctrine to be binding of all of the faithful. Hence a doctrine that the Church on earth has previously believed, but which was not binding as such on all of the faithful on pain of sin, is made binding upon them for their own spiritual good. Since this imposes an obligation on the faithful to give their assent to the doctrine itself, such a declaration can only be made either by the pope himself as the highest authority under God in the Church on earth, or by the decisions of an ecumenical council that have been formally ratified by the reigning pope. Once the doctrine has been made binding on all of the faithful in this way, it is necessary for all of the baptized under the authority of the Church on earth to give their assent to the same on pain of sin. If the doctrine once ratified does not receive the assent of any of the faithful, the individual who has withheld his assent in the given case is a heretic who places his soul at risk and can be subject to the proper disciplinary action by the authorities of the Church on earth. The third category refers to doctrines that are closely related to those that have been infallibly defined, but are not binding on the faithful in the same way. Insofar as they are consistent with what the Church on earth has solemnly defined as the doctrines of the Church on earth through the proper authorities, then it is beneficial for the faithful to assent to them even if they are not strictly binding on them. But that they are not as such binding on the faithful does mean that no sin is necessarily incurred if they are to be rejected.

      The doctrines of the Church on earth as a whole that are binding on the faithful fall into one of four different categories. First, there are the immutable doctrines of the Church on earth that have been infallibly defined either by the reigning pope or by an ecumenical council and ratified by the reigning pope. These are the infallible doctrines that were mentioned above. Second, there are the premises that go into the doctrines that have been infallibly defined, without which it is not possible to understand the immutable doctrines themselves. Third, there is the conclusions that can be derived from the immutable doctrines, and which are consistent with them. If the conclusions were not accepted, then it would undermine the integrity of the infallibly proclaimed doctrine. Fourth, there are dogmatic facts, which are historical realities that relate to the immutable doctrines, and which cannot be separated from them without undermining the doctrine. Such an example would be that Christ died on the Cross rather than by some other method of execution. It is a theological truth that Christ truly died and then rose from the dead, but the historical manner of Christ's death is a dogmatic fact that is necessarily known and accepted in order to better understand the nature of the immutable doctrines to which it relates. From this it is evident that the most important aspects of these four is the actual immutable doctrines of the Church on earth that have been infallibly defined for the good of the faithful, and to which the faithful must give their assent on pain of sin. But these other categories are necessary to know the nature of the doctrines that have been infallibly defined, meaning they cannot be rejected without failing to properly understand the doctrines and without also falling into heresy. These are all of the different categories to which the faithful must give their assent in order for them to avoid sin. There are many other doctrines in the Church on earth that have been propounded at different times over the history of the Church on earth, but they are not also binding on the faithful in the same way as these four categories. The faithful have the ability to decide for themselves on these other matters what they seek to believe. They can choose what makes the best intellectual sense to them without necessarily incurring any penalty from the Church on earth or putting their souls at risk. It is proper that the Church on earth gives the faithful some freedom about their beliefs even while she requires assent for the most essential doctrines because this freedom can help the men to better use their rational intellect and free will for the sake of forming their consciences.

The matter of the immutable doctrines of the Church on earth is necessarily related to the highest offices in the Church on earth, which have the ability to decide these matters for the good of all of the faithful in the Church on earth. Since the Church on earth in general receives her authority from Christ through the power of binding and loosing, the faithful will be held to account to what degree they obeyed the legitimate authorities of the Church on earth concerning matters of Church doctrine. If the doctrines that the Church on earth has made binding for all of the faithful are not accepted as true by the baptized, then it necessarily follows that God Himself is not properly known. If God is not known, then God cannot be properly loved, since the subject will give his love to a being that exists only in his own mind and not to the God Who actually exists and Who works to save men through the acts of Christ and His Church. This is the necessity of all of the faithful adhering to the doctrines of the Church on earth that the authorities in the Church on earth have ordered to be accepted by all of the faithful. Christ Himself said to the apostles that who hears them hears Him, meaning that when the Church authorities, as the successors to the apostles, make such decisions, the faithful ought to submit to them in the same way that they would submit to Christ Himself. This is because they stand in the person of Christ as the priesthood of the Church on earth and as the successors to the apostles.

From what has been said, it is evident that the infallible declarations that are made by the Church authorities must necessarily come either from the pope or from an ecumenical council that has been ratified by the pope. This does not mean that everything that comes either from a pope or an ecumenical council is necessarily infallible or requires the assent of belief. Most of what has been said by both of these authorities does not rise to the level of infallibility. This does not mean that these fallible statements can or ought to be disregarded, but that they are not meant to be binding on all of the faithful on pain of sin. Hence the faithful still have some latitude in deciding whether the statements made are actually true. It is not inevitable that they are true because they do not inherently carry with them the protection of infallibility that comes from the Holy Spirit Who guides the Church on earth for the good of the faithful.

Yet since these are the highest authorities in the Church on earth under God, it is necessarily the case that the decisions made by these authorities are binding on the entire Church on earth. Since there is no higher authority in the Church on earth under God than the pope himself, it is not possible to appeal to any other authority in the event that the pope makes a decision that does not appear to be correct or prudent. But at the same time that the pope is the final authority under God within the Church on earth, the pope is still bound by the decisions that were previously made in the history of the Church on earth. This means that the pope cannot do whatever he pleases so that the faithful must necessarily obey him. If a particular matter has already been settled by the Church on earth with an infallibly proclaimed doctrine, it is impossible for the pope to change what was already established. What was infallibly proclaimed is infallible because the Holy Spirit Who is God guides the

Church on earth. Since the Holy Spirit as God is infallible, it is impossible for previous decisions made with the guidance of the Holy Spirit to be overturned. This would mean that God contradicted Himself, which is impossible. Hence the pope cannot simply decide whatever he wants for the Church on earth and make it binding on the faithful. The pope must obey the decisions of the Church on earth on previous matters. Any future such declarations on matters of faith and morals must only be used to clarify what the Church on earth had always believed. This is necessarily the case because the public revelation given to the whole Church on earth ended with the death of the last of the apostles. This means that nothing new can be proclaimed that has not already been understood in some manner in the Church on earth since the beginning.

It is also necessary to consider the role of the pope in general as the highest authority in the Church on earth under God. This derives from the primacy of St. Peter among the apostles. It is evident that St. Peter was the leader of the apostles after Christ. Christ specifically referred to St. Peter as the rock upon which Christ would build the Church on earth. Christ said this in response to St. Peter's declaration of faith when Christ had asked the apostles about His identity. Christ later told St. Peter three times to feed His sheep, which meant to lead the Church on earth once Christ had ascended to the Father. St. Peter is present at all of the major events in the life of Christ, such as the Transfiguration. St. Peter was the first of the apostles to see the risen Christ. St. Peter was always referred to by others at the time as being the leader of the apostles after Christ. And the name of St. Peter always comes at the beginning of any of the different lists of the names of the apostles. From these different things, it is evident that while Christ made all of the apostles to be the first priesthood of the Church on earth, there was still an established hierarchy among them, so that St. Peter was the leader of the apostles after Christ. St. John was the apostle whom Christ had loved the most, but this does not mean that Christ did not give the supreme authority in the Church on earth after Himself to St. Peter.

      The primacy of St. Peter among the apostles continues through their successors in the priesthood down to the present day. Since St. Peter founded the Church in Rome, the bishops of Rome are all the successors to St. Peter, meaning that they have the primacy over the other bishops in the Church on earth. In the same way that St. Peter was the leader of the apostles, the pope in Rome is the leader of the rest of the Church on earth. It is very well attested within the history of the Church on earth that St. Peter and St. Paul founded the Church in Rome, and thus that Rome is the head of all of the churches in the entire world. St. Clement of Rome, St. Ignatius of Antioch, St. Polycarp of Smyrna, St. Justin Martyr, and St. Irenaeus of Lyon, among many other prelates of the Church on earth from the earliest times after the apostles, all attested to how the Church in Rome was founded by St. Peter and St. Paul, and that it is through St. Peter that Rome has the supreme authority under God over the rest of the Church on earth. Hence it is beyond doubt that St. Peter is the founder of the Church in Rome, and that the authority that Christ Himself gave to St. Peter after Himself devolves upon all of the popes since St. Peter as the bishops of Rome. And since the primacy of Rome is one of the necessary parts of the Church on earth, Rome is the only part of the Church on earth that is necessarily protected from defecting from the rest of the Church on earth. All of the other parts of the Church on earth around the world can potentially lose the faith by falling into heresy or apostasy. But since Rome is the head of all of the churches around the world, Rome is the one place that is guaranteed not to lose the faith. This does not mean that other corruption in Rome is not possible. It only means that Rome cannot totally lose the faith in the way that this is possible to the other parts of the Church on earth around the world. This is the necessity of the primacy of St. Peter which devolves upon the Roman popes throughout the history of the Church on earth. And it is necessary for the other churches around the world to be in communion with Rome in order for them to be part of the one true Church that Christ founded on earth, and which will last until the Second Coming.

The existence of the papacy and the primacy of the pope as the bishop of Rome is one of the essential characteristics of the Church on earth as Christ and the apostles had founded her. Since Rome is the one church within the entire Church on earth that cannot defect, this relates to the indefectibility of the Church on earth as well. For Rome to defect would mean that the Church on earth was lacking in a visible head, namely the pope. As the papacy itself is one of the essential characteristics of the Church on earth, the loss of the papacy would mean that the Rome had defected, which was said to be impossible.

The papacy as the visible head of the Church on earth, with Christ Himself as the invisible head of the Church because He ascended to the Father, relates to the unity of the Church on earth. That the Church on earth is one is called one of the four marks of the Church. The four marks are all characteristics that the Church on earth received from Christ and the apostles when the Church on earth was founded at the time of the First Coming.

First, the Church on earth is necessarily one because all of the baptized are bound to each other and above all to God by the Divine grace and virtue that they had received in that sacrament. This means that the Church has to be one. The faithful must all be unanimous in the most important doctrines of the faith as the way to properly know God. As it was said, if God is not properly known, God cannot be loved either. If men cannot properly love God for Who He is, they cannot come closer to God in order for them to be saved when they die. This means that they will instead go to hell and receive the just punishment for the sins that they had committed by which they had rejected God. It is likewise evident that Christ intended to found one Church on earth by how He prayed that His disciples would all be one. Just as there is one God, one Christ, one faith, and one baptism, it is necessary that there is one Church. And the one Church on earth properly has one visible head, who is the pope, who rules the Church on earth using the authority that he received from the apostles by his ordination and as the legitimate successor to St. Peter. Thus the unity of the Church on earth as one Church rather than many churches is one of the most important characteristics of the Church on earth. And since Christ sent the Holy Spirit only into the Church on earth that He had founded, no man has the authority to break from the Church on earth to establish his own institution in opposition to the Church that Christ founded on earth. This is clear from what was said.

Second, it is characteristic of the Church on earth that she is holy. Now this can be said in three ways. First, for something to be holy means that it is perfect, and the perfect lacks nothing that is possible to it as what it is. Since the Church on earth is a self-sufficient spiritual society with no need from any other institution on earth, this is one of the ways that the Church on earth can be called holy. This was already explained in greater detail when addressing the nature of the Church on earth as a perfect spiritual society. Second, the Church on earth is holy because she is the bride of Christ, and Christ loves the Church with the same love that a man has for his wife. Now love means to desire the good for the object that is loved. And since God alone is pure act, God does not desire the good for what He loves. God makes the object to be good by His essence. As Christ is both God and man within the one hypostasis, this means that Christ loves in the same manner. So Christ loves the Church by making the Church to be good. And He does this by giving His grace and virtue to the faithful in the Church on earth in order for them to be saved when they die. Thus they can come to be with God in the state of beatitude. Third, the Church on earth is holy because she is the spiritual body of Christ on earth. The Church on earth ministers to the faithful in order for them to receive the Divine grace and virtue that men need if they are to be saved when they die. Now Christ is holy above all else because He is God as well as man, meaning that Christ as God is absolutely perfect, and Christ's Divinity makes His humanity to be relatively perfect. As the Church on earth continues Christ's ministry to fallen men while Christ Himself is in heaven, this means the Church on earth is holy just as Christ is holy. Hence these are the three ways that the Church on earth is holy.

Third, the Church on earth is properly called Catholic, which means that the Church is a universal institution. What the Church on earth has established for men to be saved is binding on all men insofar as they seek to come to be with God in the state of beatitude. Christ made it so that salvation is possible to all men as such. Thus the doctrines and practices that are common to the whole Church on earth are necessary for the perfection of human nature as such. While there can be some differences in certain practices or states of life within the Church on earth, what the Church on earth upholds for all of the faithful pertains to human nature in general. This is the only way that men can be perfected as who they are through the power of Christ by Whom men can come to be with God in beatitude when they die. Similarly it is also said concerning the doctrines of the Church that the Catholic truth is what the Church on earth always taught and believed in all times and places. Such beliefs are binding on all of the faithful in the Church according to their nature as men. The faithful must give their assent to these doctrines if they are to retain the Divine grace and virtue that they had received in baptism, and to avoid falling into the sin of heresy.

Fourth, the Church on earth is apostolic, meaning that the Church on earth is necessarily faithful to what Christ and the apostles established for men to be saved. This does not mean that it is not possible for the doctrine or practices of the Church on earth to develop in certain ways over time. But the developments that take place in the history of the Church on earth are always consistent with what came before. So if some practices were different in one time from another, this does not have to mean that what came after is less than what came before. It can even be said that the doctrines of the Church on earth see their own development in some ways as well. But this can only happen so that what came after is still consistent with what came before. The later developments in the doctrines of the Church on earth are supposed to clarify what the Church always believed and understood from the very beginning. It is impossible for what came before to be contradictory with what comes after. The truth is always the same, meaning that the Church cannot change a doctrine to say that what was is no longer or that what never was now is. This would mean that the Holy Spirit Who is God and Who protects the Church on earth had contradicted Himself, and this is altogether impossible.

These are the four marks of the Church. From what has been said, it is evident that they relate to much of what has already been said concerning the nature of the Church on earth, such as indefectibility and infallibility. These characteristics of the Church on earth cannot be understood apart from the four marks of the Church. And the Church on earth possesses all of her general characteristics because of the way that Christ and the apostles established the Church on earth at the time of the First Coming. From the way that Christ sent the Holy Spirit into the Church on earth to protect her from all error, it is evident that the Church on earth will always retain her essential characteristics until the time of the Second Coming, when Christ will come to establish the kingdom of God in its fullness with the New Heaven and New Earth.

While the indefectibility and infallibility of the Church on earth primarily concern the doctrines of the Church on earth, these things also relate to the practices of the Church on earth as well. The seven sacraments, which form the core of the Church's practices, are understood in terms of the immutable doctrines of the Church on earth that make them to be what they are. Hence there is a necessary link between doctrine and practice that exists in the Church. It can even be said that the Church on earth prays as she believes. This is the principle in the Church that the law of prayer is the law of belief. First different practices in the Church on earth develop from the ways that the faithful pray. Since the Holy Spirit guides the Church on earth, the Holy Spirit guides the different ways that the faithful pray. Then once the practices of praying in the Church have been established over time, the Church will develop her theology in accord with the ways that she prays. Thus the law of prayer is the law of belief. And the primary way that the Church on earth prays to God is through the liturgy.

The liturgy of the Church on earth consists of all of the different public rites in the Church by which the Church on earth prays to God for the salvation of the world. Many of the particular liturgical practices in the Church on earth were inherited from the liturgies of ancient Judaism. The Church learned from the Old Law the proper ways for men to offer prayer to God, and adapted these different rites to the New Law. Hence the Mass, the celebration of the Eucharist as the central liturgical rite in the Church on earth, was formed by combining the ancient synagogue service with the Passover meal. In the earliest days of the Church, when most of the faithful were observant Jews, the faithful continued to attend the synagogue services on Saturday in addition to celebrating the Eucharist at the Passover meal held on Sunday as the way to commemorate the Resurrection. Then once the faithful were expelled from the synagogues following the destruction of the Temple, they would hold the synagogue service on Sunday before having the Passover meal as the way to celebrate the Eucharist. As the Church grew, the Passover meal eventually fell out of the Mass so that only the consecration of the bread and the wine remained, which were then moved together to the same time within the Mass. This is how the Mass developed into its current form. And the Mass already held this form at the time of St. Justin Martyr less than a century after the time of the apostles. Thus the Church on earth continued to use the knowledge of liturgy and the rites that were inherited from ancient Judaism to offer prayer to God. The only difference is that the rites now constituted within the Church on earth were able to adore Christ in reality rather than just in figure, which had been the case for the Jews in the time of the Old Law. Thus the rites of the Church on earth are the fulfillment of the signs and figures that had existed under the Old Law.

The Church on earth also continued other practices beyond the time of Christ which had been present in ancient Judaism. The Divine Office is the official prayer of the Church on earth, being second in importance only to the Mass as the Church's most important liturgical rite. It is evident that the Jewish people had been praying the Psalms going back at least to the time of King David, who is believed to have written many of the Psalms himself. The Jews developed the practice of praying the Psalms at different set times throughout the day in order to consecrate each part of every day to God. This was considered to be the sacrifice of praise that the Jews had offered to God along with the sacrifices of the animals that God had ordered them to make to Him in the Temple. And the sacrifice of praise had obtained a new significance when the Jews were in exile in Babylon and the Temple had been destroyed when their kingdoms were conquered. This remained at the time the only part of the Old Law that they could still practice until the Temple was eventually restored. The Jews continued to observe this practice through the time of Christ, and it was inherited by the Church on earth, since the Church continued to use the Psalms as her official prayer book. Once the First Coming had taken place, it was now possible for the faithful in the Church on earth to fully understand the references to Christ contained within the Psalms, since the things that God had predicted and promised to mankind under the Old Law were fulfilled by Christ at the time of the First Coming. Hence the Psalms retain their relevance under the New Law just as they had been significant under the Old Law. Indeed it can even be said that they are more significant under the New Law because the signs and figures in the Psalms have become a reality through Christ.

  The Church on earth likewise developed other rites in the liturgy based on the knowledge that was obtained through the practices under the Old Law. Hence all of the different sacraments are properly ministered within the context of the liturgy of the Church on earth. This way the faithful can use the signs and figures present within the liturgy to better understand the invisible reality that takes place when Christ ministers to the faithful through the different rites of the Church. As the priesthood of the Church on earth stands in the person of Christ to minister to the rest of the faithful for their sanctification, it can be said that the liturgy how Christ Himself ministers to the faithful. Since Christ works through His ordained priests in this manner, it is necessary that the faithful understand the meaning of the liturgy in order for them to be properly disposed to receive what Christ gives to men through the different rites of the Church on earth. Thus they can receive more of the Divine grace and virtue for them to come closer to God over time in the hope of eventually being saved.

It might be supposed that God does not need or desire the material goods that the faithful offer to God in the liturgy. But any material goods or the ritual acts associated with the liturgy are meant to better dispose the faithful to come to God. Hence when men offer expensive material goods to the Church on earth for their use in the liturgy, this is a way for them to show their love for God. They could potentially use their material wealth for some other purpose, but instead they chose to give to the Church for the liturgy. While God does not need or desire these things from men, God does want men to love Him for the sake of their own good. As men are composed of both soul and body, to offer material goods as a sign of love for God can better dispose the men to God so that they can receive more of His grace and virtue. Christ Himself consented to the use of material goods as a way to glorify God when He commended Mary for giving Him the expensive oil. The apostles protested that the money she spent on the oil could have been used to help the poor, but Christ told her that she did well when she gave Him the oil, because He was more important to her than anything or anyone else. Now this does not mean that a man is less virtuous if he lacks the material goods to offer to God. Christ also made this clear when He told the apostles that the elderly widow who gave her few coins had contributed more to the Temple than the wealthier men who gave a greater amount of money. The wealthier men had more to spare while the widow gave all that she had, meaning her sacrifice was greater than that of the other men. What matters is the disposition with which the men act rather than the nature of what they do when they try to offer something to God. As the psalmist had said, God told men to rend their hearts rather than their garments as the way to show God the sorrow for their former sins.

Now the liturgy of the Church on earth, as the public rites by which Christ ministers to men and the men receive the Divine grace and virtue from Christ, are based on the rites of the Old Law. Under the Old Law, God had specifically told the Jews the different ways that they were to offer their sacrifices and their prayers to Him. But since the New Law is a lesser burden to men than the Old Law, Christ did not as specifically instruct men on the ways that the rites of the Church on earth ought to be constituted. The Church on earth has always understood that there are certain core elements of the liturgy that cannot be changed. These core elements come from Christ and the apostles when they established these different rites in the Church on earth. For the most part these immutable liturgical elements concern the ministry of the seven sacraments. If the matter or the form of the seven sacraments was to be altered from what it is, then the sacrament would be invalid and the recipient would not receive the character or the Divine grace and virtue from the sacrament itself. Hence there are some elements in the liturgy itself that can never be altered at all. They are the parts of the liturgy that are of either Divine or apostolic origin. But beyond these elements, it is clear that Christ gave the Church on earth a relatively free hand in developing the liturgy itself. This is actually for the better in its own way. While this can potentially lend itself to different problems within the rites of the liturgy, the freedom of the Church to constitute most of these rites means that the rites that the Church has established are observed with greater virtue. There can be no virtue if there is no free will in the first place. As Christ allowed the Church to have more freedom in the order of the liturgy, it can be said that the establishment and the observance thereof is more virtuous for men and for the Church on earth as a whole.

Yet while the Church on earth has a relatively free hand in the order of the liturgical rites, it is still the case that the Holy Spirit guides the Church on earth in the liturgy. This is mainly so that the Church will never lose or alter the essential characteristics inherent in the different liturgical rites, such as the matter and form of the seven sacraments. This relates to the indefectibility of the Church on earth. If the Church on earth was able to lose the sacraments in this way, she would indeed have defected. As this is impossible because of the guidance of the Holy Spirit, the Church cannot lose these most essential liturgical elements in any time or place.

Time and place also influence the ways that the liturgy of the Church on earth has developed over time. While the core elements of the liturgy, both the matter and form of the seven sacraments and other general elements in the liturgy, are the same across all of time and all of the different places on earth where the Church exists, it is still the case that different ways of observing the different liturgical practices have developed in various times and places. What was done in one time and place in the liturgy may not be done in exactly the same way in another time and place. This does not mean that any one liturgical practice in a given time or place is more or less valuable than the same practice as constituted in a different time or place. But since Christ and the apostles gave the Church on earth certain latitude in the development of the liturgy, different times and places often observe the same practices in different ways. There are occasions when the various times and places had adapted different parts of the liturgical practices to suit their own particular circumstances. Since these different elements may work better in one place or another as a way for men to receive the Divine grace and virtue, the Church has allowed for such variety to take place within certain prescribed limits.

  The way that different liturgical rites developed differently from one time and place to another is a matter of some interest. It is clear that the different liturgical rites in the Church developed slowly over time by the work of many different men. Hence it has often been the case that certain private practices of devotion were later adopted into the public celebration of the liturgy, so that they became the norm for the time and place in particular where they had developed. The Church on earth has condoned and approved that these practices develop in these ways. Since the Holy Spirit guides the Church on earth in the development of the liturgy, these changes can be allowed at different times and in different places as long as they remain in accord with the sacred doctrine of the Church on earth. Thus if there is nothing heretical is incorporated into the liturgy of the Church on earth, the practices can be allowed to remain or to develop freely. It is also the case that this organic development of the liturgy means that practices that are not beneficial to the liturgy itself or to the people for whom the liturgy exists can fall out of use over time, while the ones that are more beneficial to the Church on earth will remain. This way the Church on earth can better communicate by means of the liturgical symbols the different truths that the faithful in the Church on earth all believe for the sake of their salvation. This is a natural way to add to the overall quality of the liturgy. If certain practices were not as beneficial, then they would not last a long time, while those that lasted are likely better for the Church.

Beyond the organic development of the liturgy of the Church on earth is the right of the priesthood of the Church on earth to regulate the different liturgical practices for the good of the faithful. This belongs to the power of binding and loosing that Christ gave to the apostles as the first priesthood of the Church on earth, the exercise of which is guided by the Holy Spirit. Thus if it is ever the case that any heretical beliefs are reflected in any of the different liturgical rites of the Church on earth, it is the obligation of the Church authorities to forbid such practices for the good of the faithful. It is also the case that the Church authorities can take other steps to make sure that the development of the liturgy occurs in proper order, so that different parts of the liturgy still reflect their intended purpose. Hence they can remove certain elements from parts of the liturgy or perhaps add some parts elsewhere if this better reflects the nature of the liturgical practice itself. That the Church authorities can alter the liturgy in this way is evident going back to the earliest times, such as when the Creed was added to the Mass liturgy to protect the faithful against heretical beliefs about the Trinity.

      The ability of the Church authorities to regulate liturgical matters should not be exercised lightly given the connection that exists between the law of prayer and the law of belief in the Church on earth. The liturgy is meant to express different invisible realities, and the ways that the different liturgical practices have developed over time means that the better practices have endured while the ones of lesser value have fallen away. This was explained concerning the organic development of the liturgy. Thus if the authorities of the Church on earth were to recklessly reform the liturgy of the Church on earth, this could potentially lead to great harm among the faithful. While the Holy Spirit guides the Church on earth, and such guidance does protect the liturgy in terms of certain core elements, this does not mean that every liturgical order that comes from the authorities of the Church on earth is necessarily the work of the Holy Spirit, or even that it is beneficial to the faithful in the Church on earth. Since most of the liturgy is composed of manmade elements, these elements are necessarily imperfect in their own way. So are the ways that the Church authorities regulate the functions within the liturgy. This is necessarily the case simply because these matters concern imperfect men living in the fallen world. So it does not follow that every time the Church authorities regulate the liturgy that it has to be good in itself or beneficial to the Church on earth, much less inspired by the Holy Spirit. The regulation of liturgical matters in the Church on earth is an act of prudential judgment by the Church authorities. As they are fallen men who are still capable of committing sins and doing other imperfect acts, it is possible that they could impose directives or changes to the Church's liturgy that would not be prudent or beneficial for the good of the faithful in the Church on earth.

Yet since the Church hierarchy receives its authority from Christ, any imprudent directives or changes to the Church's liturgy cannot simply be ignored on that account. This is the virtue of obedience which the faithful owe to the Church hierarchy. Obedience means to do the will of another. Men ought to obey other men in the event that the other men may know better than they do. And some men are given legitimate authority over other men so that they can have more information about what needs to be done for the good of those over whom they rule. Since they have more information by being over the other men, the other men ought to obey them even if the other men suspect that their judgment might be imprudent for the common good. It is not the task of the men bound to obedience to decide for themselves what ought to be done, since they do not have the same information as the men placed over them. It may indeed be that the men bound to obedience are correct in their belief that the men over them were imprudent in their decisions. But since they do not have the same information, they cannot be entirely sure, meaning that they are still bound to obedience to those other men. Obedience only when a man agrees with what is done does not constitute the virtue of obedience. There are some cases when the men who are bound to obedience can disobey the higher authority. This was already explained. It is possible when the higher authority himself violates an explicit law by which all of the men are bound. In which case it is necessary for the sake of virtue that the order given is not obeyed. But this is not the case in matters of prudential judgment. And most of what concerns the liturgy and different liturgical orders in the Church on earth are matters of prudential judgment. It is not for the rest of the faithful to take these matters into their own hands decide to act contrary to what the legitimate authorities in the Church on earth have ordered for the liturgy. St. Paul spoke at some length about the necessity of giving obedience to legitimate authorities, and the authority of the Church hierarchy comes from Christ Himself Who ordained the apostles as the first priesthood of the Church on earth.

Thus it is evident that not all changes or directives that come from the Church hierarchy concerning the liturgy of the Church on earth have to be either beneficial for the faithful or inspired by the Holy Spirit. The guidance of the Holy Spirit over the liturgy for the most part only relates to certain core liturgical elements, such as the matter and form of the seven sacraments. But there are indeed other ways that the Holy Spirit affects the order of the liturgy, since it was said that the law of prayer in the Church on earth is the law of belief, and the Holy Spirit guides the Church on earth to protect her from all error in her sacred doctrine. Thus there is a more limited way in which the Holy Spirit also protects the liturgy of the Church on earth through the essential connection to the Church's sacred doctrine. And while not all of the decisions made by the Church hierarchy concerning the liturgy are necessarily good, they still have to be obeyed all the same unless it is evident that there is an explicit higher law that the authorities of the Church on earth are attempting to disobey. Those orders must not be followed because an unjust law is no law at all.

While the liturgy as such is common to the entire Church on earth, and thus is necessary for all men as such to adore God and to better understand the sacred doctrine of the Church on earth, the same liturgical practices may differ from one time and place to another. This was already said. Hence the Church on earth allows at the same time both for general things that are applicable to all men as well as other particular things that take into account the different states of men in life. This way both the general and the particular for men can be better directed to God as the ultimate end for all men. It is in this way that the Church on earth has upheld the three evangelical counsels as a means to spiritual perfection for those who seek this state in life. Christ

Himself established the three evangelical counsels as a way for some men to more assiduously devote themselves to God in life for the sake of obtaining a greater reward from God in the state of beatitude. Christ told the rich man that if he wanted to seek Him more closely, he needed to sell all that he had, give to the poor, and follow Christ. Christ also said elsewhere that the state of virginity is a higher state for men than being married. This set the precedent for the three evangelical counsels of poverty, chastity, and obedience. If men want to lead a life of spiritual perfection so that they can better love God, they must live in this manner in accord with what Christ said.

First, material poverty means that men have only the most necessary material goods that they need for the sake of their survival and their delight. This does not have to mean that the men are materially deprived, since material deprivation can also possibly be the cause of spiritual harm for men as well. If a man chooses to live in a materially deprived state, he might devote more of his time and effort to seeking the material goods that he needs or developing an inordinate desire for the material goods that he does not possess. In either case the man is distracted from God to Whom he has chosen to more strictly devote himself. The man cannot give as much to God in this state as he would if he had more of the necessary material goods for the sake of his survival. In which case it is better for men to have some material goods in life to meet their needs. Once their material needs have been met in this way, they can better focus the mind more on God in order to give to God more of the love that He deserves from them. But at the same time, Christ said that it is easier for a camel to pass through the eye of a needle than for a rich man to enter heaven. If men have many material goods, they will derive more delight from them so that they have less of an appetite for the higher spiritual goods that God gives to men in life. They will also have to give more time and effort to manage all of their material goods, meaning that they will have less time to spend with God in prayer. These are two of the reasons why material wealth is dangerous for men in a spiritual sense. Thus it is better for men to have only the most necessary material goods in life for their survival and their delight. This way they can devote themselves more fully to God for the spiritual goods that He can give them in life and the ones that they hope to obtain from Him in the state of beatitude.

Second, chastity in this case means that a man is not married and does not engage in any sexual activity outside of marriage. This was already addressed concerning how Christ said that it is better for a man to remain alone because this way he can be devoted more directly to God rather than devoted to God through his wife. And the apostles concurred with Christ in this matter even before Christ told them the truth. For which reason it is necessary for spiritual perfection that men remain unmarried and do not engage in any sexual activity. This is also the case because the sexual passions that are possible to men are the strongest passions that men can experience in life. Since men are fallen, their passions do not always follow the direction of the rational intellect and free will. So it is better for men to maintain order in their lives by refraining altogether from sexual activity. This way the men cannot be more easily moved by their passions. Their sexual passions will become weaker over time because of the way that the men have refused to gratify them. And since they have also learned to control their passions in this manner at the same time, this frees them to better devote themselves to God above all else.

Third, obedience, as it was said, means that the subject chooses to do the will of another. This is actually the most important of the three evangelical counsels because it is the one that contains the others. When observing the three evangelical counsels, the subject obeys not only God above all else, but also his human superiors whose task it is to help him do the will of God.

This way he recognizes that he does not know that can be known in order to work for the sake of his own good, meaning that he will submit to other men who ought to know better. The spiritual benefit of doing the will of another means that the obedient man does not have to use his own rational intellect and free will in every case to make decisions about how to act. Thus he is free to focus more on God through the works that he does in accord with obedience. At the same time, to obey other men is an act of humility, since the man who obeys does not assume that he is better than other men if he is willing to subject himself to their authority. Since humility is the opposite of pride, where pride is the origin of all other sins, the humble man must lack all sins if he lacks pride. If the cause is removed, so is the effect. This means that humility can be taken as being the same as all virtue, and obedience to legitimate authority helps men to be humble before God and their fellow man. It can even be said that obedience itself is the same as all virtue, since the virtuous man does the will of God above all else. As God does all that He does in every case for the sake of the greatest possible good, this means that all acts of virtue can be reduced to obeying God's will, meaning that obedience can be taken as being the same as all virtue. And among the three evangelical counsels, obedience is the greatest of the three because it contains the others.

Thus it is evident that poverty, chastity, and obedience are the way for men to attain to a state of spiritual perfection. Men can understand this because Christ Himself stated the same, and the observance of these three counsels can bring men closer to God by the ways that they allow men to clear their minds from created distractions in order to focus more on God Himself. This way men can lead a life dedicated to God in prayer. This is the nature of the different religious orders that exist in the Church on earth.

The state of religion in the Church is so called because religious bind themselves through their vows more closely to God in order for them to merit a greater reward from God in the state of beatitude when they die. Not all religious in the Church on earth take the same three vows in accord with the three evangelical counsels. But even if they are not all strictly bound by the same vows, they are all still called to live according to them for their own spiritual good. This means that it would not be proper for someone in religion to have great material wealth or to transgress by either letter or spirit what is required of him by the three evangelical counsels. This would mean that he did not live up to his state of life and he may have even violated the vows that he made when he entered into that state in the first place. This would be a great offense against God. The man would have bound himself to live in a certain way by his own free will, and then ignored the vows he made to God by which he promised to live that way. Since he broke the promise that he made to God in his vows, this would indeed be a very severe sin. In the event that no vows were broken, for the man to commit himself to live in this way and then violate his way of life would still be an insult to God. As St. Paul said, the letter kills but the spirit gives life.

Now the earliest religious in the Church on earth were the hermits. These were individual men and women who sought of their own initiative to serve God more deeply than what is required of all of the baptized in the Church on earth as such. Hence these men fled into the wilderness, into the deserts of places like Egypt and Syria, in order to pursue their devotion to God in solitude. That they left behind human society was not done out of any contempt for fallen men, but rather because the goods that they could receive if they had remained in society with other men would possibly distract them from God. Through the pursuits of the earliest hermits in the desert, they attained to great holiness. As their reputation for sanctity spread throughout the rest of the Church on earth, more men sought to live as they did. But not all of these men were able to live in the same solitude of the original hermits. Hence they eventually relaxed the aspect of solitude for their vocation so that they could live in community with other religious. This way they would all have the support of each other even though they were all set apart from the rest of human society. This is how the religious orders in the Church on earth initially developed out of their obedience to Christ through the three evangelical counsels.

All of the religious in the Church on earth share in common that they lead lives of prayer. The three evangelical counsels serve to clear out the distractions of the individuals who follow them so that they can be more strictly devoted to God in prayer. This is the primary function of all of the religious in the Church on earth, before and beyond any other work that they might do for their sanctification. But while religious as such are directed to lead a life of prayer, some of them also have charisms through which they perform certain good works in addition to prayer for the sake of their sanctification. Thus there is a distinction that emerged among the religious orders between the more active and the more contemplative of the orders. The more contemplative orders do not have a special charism of work by which they seek to better serve God. They devote themselves to God through their prayer, so that any work that they do is merely for the sake of their material survival. It is still incumbent upon religious in contemplative orders to work, since this is binding on all men by their nature. Yet in their case their work is not essentially a means to their sanctification. The more active orders still pray, but then also use their good works in the service of their fellow man to better add to their sanctity. And the Church on earth has approved and benefitted greatly from such endeavors over the course of her history.

When comparing the contemplative and the active orders within the Church on earth, it is evident that the contemplative orders occupy a higher place in the Church. This is because the contemplative orders seek God directly as their only end, while the active orders seek God more indirectly through their good works in service to their fellow man. The end is the reason for the means being so, since the means cannot be what it is except for the end to which it is directed. And God alone is the ultimate end for all things because He alone is essentially good, as being is the same thing as goodness and the Divine essence is existence Itself. So what comes closer to God in the end is greater than what is more remote from Him. As the contemplative comes to God more directly, his way of life is better than the active life. But at the same time, since there are different kinds of men both in general and in the Church on earth, not all men are called to the contemplative life, just as not all men are called to be in the state of religion in general. So while the contemplative life is the better state for men, and religion itself is better than being married or in the secular state, this does not mean that all men must live in the higher of these different states. As Christ said, if the whole body was the eye, there would be no hearing, which means that all of the men in the Church on earth serve valuable roles for the good of the whole Church. The contemplatives have a more valuable role to play from their stricter devotion to prayer, but the active orders also serve a valuable role at the same time for the Church in their own particular ways. It can also be said that while the contemplative is better than the active and religion is better than being married or in the secular state, this does not have to mean that all of the men in the higher states necessarily love God more than those in the lower ones. The higher states have a greater possibility to love God more by how they live, but this does not have to happen in every case. A man in a higher state can sin more and suffer from worse corruption relative to his state when he is compared to a man in a lower state who leads a more virtuous life and loves God through the work that he does in his state of life. It may also be that God may even choose some men from the lower states to be among the elect while some of the men in the higher states might not be chosen in the same way. The higher states are supposed to lead men more closely to God, but this does not have to happen in every single case. It depends upon the individual men, the will of God for them, and how these two things relate to each other in the particular case.

The general law of the Church is that anything possible to men that is not inherently sinful is permitted to the faithful for the sake of their sanctification. Hence the Church on earth did not have to tell the hermits in the deserts of Egypt and Syria to lead those lives. They chose to lead them on their own initiative, and the Church later chose to recognize their way of life because it was evident that it was a means to great sanctity for the men who were called to live in that way. The same was the case for the religious orders once they developed out of the eremitic life. Since the ultimate law in the Church is the salvation of souls, and these different kinds of vocations in the Church on earth have proven themselves by their results to lead men closer to God, it thus makes sense that the Church authorities give their approval to these different states or life or religious orders. This does not strictly mean that any such person who seeks to live in these ways or to form such a community necessarily needs the approval of the Church on earth to do what he does. Provided that he commits no sins, and does not presume to have the approval of the Church on earth when he does not have it, then he is free to do as he pleases in order to better serve God according to his own abilities. So it is still possible in the Church on earth for individual men to form religious orders or to live as hermits if they believe that God has called them to do so. This can be a way for them to attain to greater sanctity and to help other men do the same.

From what has been said, it makes sense that the Church on earth recognizes the different states of life that are possible to men within the context of the whole Church. The rules that are binding on all of the faithful as such pertain to human nature. But there is more in men than just human nature, since there are different ways that men can act for the sake of the good based on their own individual abilities. When some men have abilities or talents similar to those of other men, it makes sense that these men can work together for their common good and use their abilities and talents for the sake of coming closer to God in the Church on earth. That there are many different roles in the Church on earth was mentioned by St. Paul when he said that there are many gifts in the same spirit. And the existence of these different roles in the Church on earth mean that the Church in this way is a more perfect society, because there are many different roles that she can offer to men where they can use their abilities and talents more for the common good of the whole Church on earth. Hence the Church as a whole becomes holier through the different ways that the faithful can work to come closer to God. They can add to their Divine grace and virtue in these ways in the possibility that they can receive from God a greater reward in the state of beatitude.

One of the other functions of law that pertains to the Church as well is that of punishment. It was stated that the four general functions of law are to command, to permit, to prohibit, and to punish. And it has been shown throughout that the Church on earth, as a spiritual society that is endowed with the ability to make laws, exercises these different functions. There are times when the Church either commands or prohibits men for the sake of their own good, and times when the Church permits men to do as they please by their own free will for the sake of their own good. Yet when men transgress the laws of God and the Church who is guided by the Holy Spirit, it is also proper that the Church punishes men for these acts. The punishments that the Church can impose on the faithful for their transgressions are intended for the faithful to make up to God and to the rest of the Church when they have done something wrong, as well as to convince the faithful not to do the same in the future that they did in the past when they committed the transgression. Hence this can be considered an act of both justice and mercy by the Church to punish the faithful when they violate the laws of God and the Church on earth. It is justice because their suffering from the punishment allows them to make up by their good will for the evil that was done, and it is mercy because the Church seeks to prevent the men from doing the evil in the future. The men themselves were evil insofar as they had transgressed the law of the Church, which means that they did not deserve the good. But since the punishment comes as a warning to them, and the warning can get them to avoid future sins, the punishment is good in this way. Hence they received an undeserved good, which is how this is an act of mercy.

This can even be said in terms of the most severe punishment that the Church on earth can impose upon men, which is excommunication. Thus the individual man who committed a grave sin is cut off from the Divine grace and virtue in the Church on earth that comes to men from the seven sacraments. This is done as an extreme measure for the subject to repent of his sins and return to the fold of the Church on earth. And if the man does not repent and rejoin the fold of the Church because he is obstinate in his sins, then it is better for the Church as a whole that he is no longer among the faithful because of the way that he is an obstinate sinner. Yet as long as the man lives, he can still repent of his sins and come back into the fold of the Church on earth. Since the Church on earth works above all to save souls, the reason for excommunication is above all to bring men back into the fold from which they had already separated themselves by some grave sin. The severity of the penalty of excommunication is such that it should only be used in the most severe and most obstinate of cases so that the man who suffers this penalty can better understand the gravity of the sin that he committed for which he had been excommunicated from the Church. Thus it is the nature of excommunication, and indeed the other penalties in the Church on earth, that they are both intended to be retributive and rehabilitative. They are a way for the sinner to pay back to God and the Church for his sins and a way for him to learn to avoid more such sins in the future by what he does. Subject to the power of binding and loosing, the Church authorities can determine what constitutes a just penalty for different sins or crimes in the Church.

From what has been said, it is evident that there are two different parts of the Divine law, namely the Old Law and the New Law. God gave the Old Law to the Jews as the way to prepare fallen mankind to receive Christ in the New Law. And it is from Christ in the New Law that men can receive the Divine grace and virtue that they need if they are to be saved when they die. This way men can come to be with God in the state of beatitude. And what happened in the time of the Old Law was a figure of the reality that occurs under the New Law. Hence the Temple sacrifices and the other rites of the Jews under the Old Law all prefigured the way that Christ under the New Law would give men the Divine grace and virtue by His death on the Cross and His rising from the dead. Once men have united themselves to Christ on the Cross by the power of the seven sacraments of the Church on earth, they can possibly be saved when they die. The seven sacraments all serve different purposes for which men need the Divine grace and virtue, meaning that men can receive the Divine grace and virtue for the first time in baptism, be sustained in the Divine grace and virtue by the Eucharist, and return to the Divine grace and virtue by the sacrament of Penance. The other sacraments also allow men to receive the Divine grace and virtue in various ways and for the sake of different purposes. Hence all of the faithful in the Church are united through Christ and also to each other by the Divine grace and virtue that God gives to men for them to be saved. As the Church on earth is a spiritual society, it is proper that she is ruled by spiritual authorities who receive their powers from Christ Himself. Since the Church on earth works for the salvation of souls, it is proper to all of the baptized to obey the orders of the Church authorities for the sake of their own good. And since the Holy Spirit guides the Church on earth as a whole for the sake of her own good, the faithful who obey the Church authorities for the sake of their own benefit can come closer to God over time in the hope of being saved. Where the different temporal societies have as their end the acquisition of material goods, the end for the Church on earth is God Himself to Whom all of the faithful seek to obtain. Hence the faithful willingly subject themselves to God through the Church on earth so that they can work towards the experience of the greatest delight possible to them from God in the state of beatitude.

CHAPTER V.
HUMAN LAW

Since man is naturally a social animal, it belongs to men to live with other men in a society. One man on his own cannot survive in the same manner as many men working together for their common good. This is how men form societies among them for their survival and delight. This was already addressed when treating the natural law. Men all have a natural autonomy that comes to them from God, Who gave men their rational intellect and free will in the first place. But for the sake of order and the good of all of the men in the society, they choose some men from among them to be their rulers, and give up some of their natural autonomy as the price of living among the other men and working together with those men for their common good. This is the way that men form temporal states. The temporal state is the authoritative body set over the whole society to work for the material good of the men within the society itself. And since the power of the temporal state comes from men giving up some of their own natural autonomy to the temporal rulers, it can be said that the authority of the temporal state comes from God through the people themselves as the origin of the temporal state. So while Christ as God made man gave men the Church on earth as the way for men to work for their spiritual good, the temporal state has its origin in the men themselves. Men properly use their free will to create the temporal state.

Thus the temporal state is the work of the different men in their society coming together for the common good of all of the men in the society itself. And since the temporal state's authority comes through the men in the society giving the temporal state the ability to rule them, it can thus be said that the temporal state itself is the product of the free will of the men who made it. The temporal state exists because the men in the society consented to be ruled in this way. Now it is not strictly necessary for the power of the temporal state that each and every man in the society itself give his consent to be ruled in this way. While it is impossible to say for sure how the first temporal states were formed, it is most likely that they developed organically. Hence all of the different men in the society did not give and did not have to give their express consent to be ruled in certain ways. It was enough that they thought to obey the authorities that emerged or did not contest the ability of the temporal authority to issue orders for them to obey.

Insofar as the temporal state is the result of the collective will of the men in the society, what makes the authority of the temporal state to be legitimate in the first place is the popular will of the people to obey it. Yet at the same time, it is not strictly the case that all of the men in the society have to give their consent to be bound by the decisions of the temporal rulers. Hence if one man chooses not to act in accord with what the temporal rulers had ordered, this in itself does not undermine the legitimacy of the temporal state, as if the temporal state automatically lost its ability to make laws and rules for the people in the society. If one or even many men in the society choose not to follow the laws or rules enacted by the society itself, this means that their acts are criminal in some sense. It does not mean that the temporal state is no longer legitimate. For a temporal state to lose its legitimacy to rule over the men in the society must be the collective result of the men in the society deciding not to be so bound anymore. This can happen in different ways, some of which will be considered later when dealing with the concept of revolutions.

So while the authority of the temporal state is the product of the free will of the men in the society, it is also at the same time the result of their collective will to bind themselves as a society to be so ruled. The loss of such consent from one or even many men does not mean as a matter of course that the temporal state loses its authority and that the people themselves are no longer bound by its laws and rules.

Now the ability of men to form temporal states is itself the product of men to make laws and rules in the first place. Since all of the men choose to give up some of their autonomy to the temporal rulers as the price of their survival and delight in life, it can be said that some men ruling over other men is not a natural event in the sense that some men were made by their very nature to be rulers while other men were meant only to be ruled. In a natural sense, all men have the same autonomy because they are each endowed with a rational intellect and free will. Thus they can all make decisions on their own for the sake of their own good, meaning that one man is no less capable as a man to work for his own good when compared to another man. Yet it can be said that some men ruling over other men is natural insofar as it conduces to the common good of the men in the society, and men are naturally social because one man cannot survive on his own without the help of other men. Since it is natural for men to live in societies in this way, it is also natural for men to form temporal states to organize them for their own good. This is how the temporal state is a naturally occurring institution in human society. It is inevitable that some men will be placed over other men to look after the common good. And those men, because they have more information about the common good by how they are set over others, can better direct the other men for the common good for which all of the men work each in his own way. That the temporal state is the result of human free will does not mean that it is unnatural for that sense. It is natural because it conduces to other things that are within human nature, even if it is not inevitable that a man lives under the authority of one or another kind of temporal state for the sake of his own good.

It can be said that men are naturally endowed with the ability to make laws. It was said that a law in general is a precept that is promulgated by someone with legitimate authority and is meant to uphold the common good for those who are bound by it. Now the rational intellect of men can understand universal things, which means that men can understand the nature of the good as abstracted from different particular objects. Hence men can say what is the nature of the good, meaning that they can also say how the good itself relates to different material goods that are necessary for a society to survive and for its members to have some degree of delight.

Similarly, since men can make complex distinctions by the power of the rational intellect, men can learn what is the greatest possible good in each case in terms of the common good for the men in the society. Hence men can form laws and rules binding the men in the society so that they can better work for the sake of the greatest possible good for the society. And the temporal ruler, by being set over the other men in the society, has the information to see what needs to be done in the interest of the common good. So he can direct more of the men within the society to do one or another kind of act so that the whole society under his care may benefit from what was done. And they were able to know what to do because they had temporal rulers who issued laws and rules for the sake of the common good that they were meant to uphold by the power that the society gave them. Thus it is evident that men are naturally endowed with the ability to make laws.

For the good of the society itself, it is necessary that there are several characteristics in the laws that are made. First, it was said earlier that human laws are necessarily bound by the different kinds of higher law by which men are also bound at the same time. These higher laws are the natural law and the Divine law, both of which come from God, but in different ways.

Now it is the essence of law that it is for the sake of a good. And all that God does is always good because being is the same thing as goodness and the Divine essence is existence Itself. Hence God alone is essentially good, meaning that all that God does is always good, since the effect must be in the cause in order for it to be the effect of that cause. So the natural law and the Divine law, both of which come from God each in their own way, are for the sake of the greatest possible good in every case. Thus human laws must be in accord with either the natural law or the Divine law to be for the sake of the greatest possible good as well. As law is for the sake of the good as the end thereof, and things are defined by their ends, a human law that is not for the sake of the good cannot be a law, as the end thereof is not the good. This means that the law does not meet the definition of a law. Thus it can be said that an unjust law is no law at all.

Second, it is necessary that a law that is promulgated by a legitimate authority is made public to the people who are bound by the law itself. This is how the law ought to be promulgated. It is not possible for the temporal state to expect men to follow a law that they do not know exists in the first place. What is in the free will of a man is necessarily in the rational intellect before it affects the free will. Hence men cannot be expected to obey a law that that they do not know exists. This means that a secret or unknown law is contradictory to the premise of a law, since the law is issued by the authority in order for it to be obeyed. And it would be gravely unjust to punish men for failing to obey a law that they did not know they had to obey. It is the case that men cannot claim that they were ignorant of a law in order for them to escape from being punished for transgressing the law, since then any man accused of a crime would be excused on the claim that he did not know that what he did was illegal. But at the same time, the temporal state must make the laws publicly known in its own way if the temporal state intends for the law itself to be obeyed.

Third, the law that is enacted by the legitimate authority ought to be made intelligible to the people who are bound by it. It is possible that the authority could make the existence of a law known to the people who are to be bound by it, but then the people will have no understanding of the way that they are bound. It would likewise be unreasonable for the authority to expect the people to be held to a law that they cannot even understand. For this reason it is best that the laws of the temporal state are issued in a language that is widely known among the men in the society. This can be a vernacular language, or it can be a non-vernacular language that is used for particular purposes but is still understood by the people whom the law is intended to bind. Similarly it can be said that the content of the law itself that is enacted ought to be clear and simple so that the meaning of the law is not difficult for men to realize. If it was difficult in this way, then the temporal state might unjustly punish men for their disobedience. They might disobey the law not out of any evil will, but because they did not understand what was required of them in the first place.

Fourth, it is best that the laws that are enacted are written in a fairly general language for the sake of covering many different particular cases. This way the law can have a wider impact for the sake of the good that the law is meant to uphold. Now it is impossible for any human law to cover all cases in which it may be applied. And it is also possible that there will be some cases where the law is applied but the outcome of the application is not for the sake of the good that the applicable law had intended. For which reason the authority that makes the law should take into account the various ways that the law is worded so that the outcome will be the good that was intended, and so that men will not be unduly harmed because the law was not worded carefully enough when it was enacted.

These are the different qualities that can be considered when the temporal state makes new laws to uphold the common good for the whole society. In addressing the nature of human laws, it is also necessary to consider the nature of the temporal state itself that makes the laws for the respective human societies. It is evident that there are many different kinds of political constitutions that have existed in various times and places throughout history. Hence a careful consideration of the different kinds of political constitutions can be made in order to see how it is that the men in the temporal society can better work for the sake of their own good. Now since there are different kinds of political constitutions that exist among men, it is the case that some of them will necessarily be better or worse than others in different ways. This is in accord with the natural hierarchy of things that exist within the created world. Hence it is inevitable that some kinds of political constitutions will necessarily be better than others. Yet at the same time, it can be said that different societies all have different needs based on their particular circumstances. So while some political constitutions are necessarily better or worse than others, it is not the case that all different temporal states in all different times and places can be governed by the same kind of political constitution. For example, it is the case that some societies might require a stronger authority at the head of the society itself to maintain order. In another society, the authority at the head of the society can be weaker because the people can better manage their own affairs without involving the powers that rule them. Much of this depends upon time and place, but it also depends upon the particular temperaments of different peoples. To apply the political constitution of one temporal state to a very different kind of society would likely have negative results for the people in the society. On that basis it is best for different states to develop their own political constitutions rather having them imposed on them by another state. If one temporal state seeks to imitate another, this may work better, but even then it can be necessary to adapt certain characteristics to the new society for the temporal state formed to better work for the common good.

The different kinds of temporal states that are possible to men can be classified according to the number of the rulers in the state itself. Thus if the final authority in the state is one man, a few men, or many men is how the different states can be separated from each other. A state that is ruled by one man is a monarchy. A state that is ruled by a few men is an aristocracy. A state that is ruled by many men is a timocracy.

But in order for any of these three kinds of political constitutions to work well for the society that they are meant to rule, it is always necessary that the men who rule have proper virtue. This means that they do not use their power for selfish reasons, but instead for the sake of the common good that is the reason why they have their power over the other men in the society in the first place. It is also necessary that the rulers of the society especially have the virtue of prudence, meaning that they are able to do things well. A man may be personally virtuous in his own life, but this does not mean that he is also capable of ruling over other men. The ruler must learn to use discretion when he rules over other men so that he can move them to act for the sake of the greatest possible good for the whole society. In this way it is better that the ruler also has a decent understanding of human nature. Thus when he deals with other men or issues orders to them for the good of the society, he can present his orders to them in a way that shows that he is concerned for their good rather than just for his own personal good. This way he can move them more freely to obey his will. They can be confident that he will issue laws and rules for their good rather than just to exploit his power for the sake of his own personal benefit.

Hence it is impossible for a society to be well-ordered if the men who rule the society do not have proper virtue in general and some of the particular skills that men need for them to rule over other men. Many of these skills can be considered part of the virtue of prudence, as it was said. There is no way that any political constitution can ever be expected to work well in the event that the rulers in the temporal state lack proper virtue. Thus virtue is the only way that a society can be protected from corrupt rulers. And if the society as a whole does not value proper virtue, it is unlikely that the rulers will be any different. The rulers of the temporal state come from the society they rule, meaning that they will think and act in the same way as the people whom they rule. Hence the overall quality of the temporal state's functioning and the laws and rules produced will all suffer if the men in the society do not care about virtue. In those cases, there is no protection that any system can provide to the people in the society from their own rulers, because evil rulers will simply disregard the system and do what they please for their own selfish reasons. It will be immaterial to them if the men within the society who are subject to them suffer more or less because they misuse their power for their own reasons rather than using it for the common good.

There are ways that the three different kinds of political constitutions that were mentioned can become corrupted so that the temporal state as a whole does not work for the greater good of the men subject to its authority. When a monarchy becomes corrupt, it becomes a tyranny, where the ruler over the temporal state uses his power for his own sake rather than for the sake of the common good. When an aristocracy becomes corrupt, it becomes an oligarchy. Rather than the ruling men having power over the temporal state because of their wisdom or experience, the men who have the most money will use their money to rule over the other men. Thus they will use their powers to further add to their money at the expense of the rest of the society. When a timocracy becomes corrupt, it turns into a democracy. Rather than many men being able to participate in the political process because of merit, all of the men in the society will be allowed to participate, so that the will of the majority of men will always prevail rather than the will of the men whose beliefs and acts can work more efficiently for the common good of the whole society. Given that most men are evil, to allow all men to participate in the ruling of the society will mean that the will of the good men will be overridden by the will of evil men, and the society as a whole will suffer. Most men do not have the ability to even rule over their own lives, meaning it is not proper for them to have any influence over the operation of the temporal state. There is no way they can consistently work for the common good of all of the men within the society.

Thus virtue is the only way that men can be sure that they will have a good temporal state where the rulers act for the sake of the common good rather than for their own selfish reasons. But it can still be said that some states are more effective at what they do compared to other states. The general rule is that the more men who are given a share in ruling over the society, the less efficient the ruling of the society itself. One man can take more decisive acts for the sake of the common good than a few men, and a few men can take more decisive acts than many men. The more men who are involved, the more likely it is that there will be discord among them about what needs to be done. This means that the temporal state as whole will be slower and less efficient when ruling over the society. Thus it is evident from this that monarchy is the most effective political constitution because one man cannot disagree with himself, meaning that having one man rule over the society as the ultimate authority will be more effective than the men in the other kinds of political constitutions. And an aristocracy will do better than a timocracy because fewer men will have fewer disagreements among them than many men if the many men are called to participate in the operation of the temporal state.

That a monarchy is the most effective form of government means it is the best form of government. But if a monarchy becomes corrupt, it becomes the worst form of government. Monarchy is most effective, but the monarch can use his powers for either good or evil. Hence if the monarch is good, the temporal state that he rules will benefit all the more. But if he becomes a tyrant, the state will suffer more. As an aristocracy is less effective than a monarchy, an oligarchy cannot do as much damage as a tyranny, but it can do more damage than a democracy. Hence the best of governments, namely monarchy, becomes the worst of governments when corrupt, namely tyranny. The least of the good governments, namely timocracy, becomes the best of the bad governments, namely democracy. And aristocracy and oligarchy are still in the middle concerning the different forms government in their good or bad forms.

The ways that the authorities in the temporal state receive their power is another aspect to be considered. It is possible either that the people of the society can choose the leaders of the temporal state on their own, or power can be inherited by the people who rule over the rest of the society. Both of these means to power have their own respective benefits for the society. If the virtuous men within the society choose the rulers in some way, they can better work for the common good by choosing the men who know more about what needs to be done for the whole society. Hence to elect the rulers of the temporal state might work better in some cases. But it may be better in other cases for the authority of the temporal state to be inherited in some way. If people inherit the temporal power over the society from those who came before them, they can trained from youth to assume the power when they succeed to it. This way they can understand better what needs to be done compared with men who had no such training and were chosen by other men from among the rest of the men in the society. If the power is inherited, the incumbent rulers can teach their heirs how they are to rule, so that the knowledge acquired by many rulers over a long period of time is at the disposal of the heir at the time that he succeeds to power. This way he can benefit the society much better than if he was elected by the society itself in some way.

The difference among the three different kinds of temporal states is based on who is the highest authority within the temporal state. It is inevitable in any state or institution that there will always be some authority that is above all of the others, and who for the purposes of the system, cannot be wrong. This means that it is not possible to appeal beyond the final authority simply because the authority is final. Hence this authority is infallible only because it is final, rather than being final because it is infallible. This was already considered when treating the role of infallibility within the Church on earth. But the same concept applies no less to temporal states. For example, in a monarchy the final authority is the monarch. So when the monarch makes a decision about what is to be done, it is not possible to appeal beyond the monarch to some higher authority. It was said that the temporal state receives its authority from God, as Christ attested when He said that Pontius Pilate would have no power over Him if it had not been given to Pilate from above. This means that the final authority within the temporal state is still bound by the higher forms of law, namely the natural law and the Divine law. No authority in the temporal state can act contrary to these higher laws to which they are also bound at the same time and to the same degree as the men they rule. But in matters that fall under their discretion, they are final and infallible within the context of the system. So when the final authority in the temporal state is one man, the temporal state is a monarchy, while if it is a few men or many men, it is either an aristocracy or a timocracy, as it was already explained.

Hence it is evident that there is a clear distinction among the different kinds of temporal states that men can legitimately create by their own power. The fewer the number of men who exercise the final authority over the temporal state, the more effective the state at doing what needs to be done. Now Aristotle, who came up with these distinctions among the different temporal states in the first place, also proposed that the best form of government for a temporal state would be one that combined the three different kinds of good governments into one. Thus Aristotle said that the best temporal state would be a combination of a monarchy, an aristocracy, and a timocracy. In this way it is best if the final authority in the state is a monarch who can take decisive action for the common good of the people over whom he rules. But then he can also take advice from a group of aristocrats who can tell him the best way to work for the common good according to their advanced knowledge when compared to the other men in the society at large. There can also be a small class of ordinary men who can convey to the rulers on behalf of the ruled what needs to be done for the common good of the temporal state, including the vast majority of men who are not represented in this system, and who are incapable of positively contributing to the functioning of the temporal state. This way the temporal state can better work for the common good of all of the different men within the society.

There is also a case to be made that this order that Aristotle had described combining the three good forms of government is the most natural order for a temporal state. At least within the context of European states, it is evident that most of the different states that developed over time had this particular order. While some of the men in those temporal states were familiar with what Aristotle had said about the combination of the three good forms of government, this did not appear to affect the way that the different temporal states in Europe had all ordered themselves. Over time they came to organically develop governments that largely resembled what Aristotle had said. Thus there was the distinction of the three estates of the realm all under a monarch. The clergy and the nobility were the aristocrats of the realm, and the commons were the men selected from within a limited franchise to share in the operation of the temporal state as well. While the system of the three estates did not operate in the same ways in all of the different temporal states across Europe, it is evident that this structure was common to most of them. Even temporal states that otherwise bore little resemblance to each other and did not influence each other very much all came to be ruled in approximately the same manner. They all formally gave their recognition to the men within these societies according to their distinction among the three different estates. Since all of this appeared to develop organically over time without any direct influence from what Aristotle had earlier proposed, there is good reason to suppose that this is the most natural order for the temporal state. There have also been other temporal states outside of Europe that developed along the same lines.

Much has been said here about the ways that the different temporal states operate for the good of the societies that they are meant to rule. And it was said that the different constitutions of the temporal states of Europe all developed along roughly the same lines. In the end they all followed the basic order that Aristotle proposed for the temporal state even though they were not established with direct reference to what he said. They all happened to develop in this way. This relates to how the constitution of the temporal state can be either written or unwritten. Most of the temporal states in human society developed over time and were not enshrined in a particular document meant to commemorate their operation. They developed so that the people in the temporal state often did the same things in the same or similar ways, so that the ways that they did things became prescriptive over time. Hence certain customs of the temporal state that were not well-established at an earlier time might be more easily transgressed at that time than they would be at a later time when the custom was much better established. The same transgression might be pardonable at one time but inexcusable at another. Yet since the temporal state itself became well-established over time along certain lines, it is not strictly necessary for the temporal state to codify its operation in a single document. This can also allow the temporal state to continue to develop over time, so that what was not suitable for the temporal state at one time may be so for another. Thus the continuity of the temporal state is thereby upheld, which adds to the stability of the society as a whole.

But it may also be the case that the constitution of the state can be codified. This can be done either through many documents, as it is in some temporal states, or it can be done using one document that explains the ways that the temporal state is meant to rule over the rest of the society. This can make matters clearer for the men in the temporal state and in the society as a whole about what is permissible concerning the operation of the temporal state. Yet at the same time, the codification of the temporal state in either one or more documents might prevent the temporal state from organic development so that the state can better work over time to uphold the common good. Some of the codified practices of the temporal state might become obsolete or even harmful over time because of the way that the circumstances within the society changed. It can be better for a temporal state to have a customary constitution rather than a codified constitution. Which of these is better for a particular state is a matter of discretion. Some societies may require a codified constitution while other societies can work well without one. The customs that developed over time can be enough for the temporal state to work for the common good of the people over whom they rule.

While every temporal state necessarily has some final authority, who for the purposes of the system is infallible because it is impossible to appeal beyond him, this does not mean that all of the authority within the temporal state is directly exercised by the final authority. Aristotle distinguished the three good forms of government and the three bad forms of government, and it is clear that the abuse of the temporal state produces the bad forms of government. Hence a monarchy, as the best form of government, degenerates into a tyranny, which is the worst form of government. A tyranny differs from a monarchy in that while the monarch is the final authority within the temporal state, the tyrant is the only authority in the temporal state. It is also the case that a tyranny differs from a monarchy because the tyrant works only for his own good while the monarch works for the common good. The same can be said for the distinctions between the other good and bad forms of government. The bad forms of government are such because the rulers within them all work for their own good rather than for the common good, and they are all willing to go beyond the proper limits of their power for the sake of their own good at the expense of the common good. Since the rulers in the bad forms of government all lack proper virtue, they have no reason to respect the political constitution of the temporal state. They will do all that they can do to work for their own good regardless of the effects that this may have for the rest of the people over whom they rule.

There is another matter to be addressed concerning the rule of the temporal state. This is the degree to which the temporal state itself may exercise its authority over the people within the society. It can generally be said that a temporal state that does less for its own people and leaves the people to work more for their own good is better than a state that tells the people what to do on more occasions. The temporal state exists for the sake of the common good, and men work for the sake of their own good by proper virtue. But proper virtue is possible to men only when they have free will. The man who more freely does the good is better than the man who acts less freely. The former is more the cause of his own good, meaning he becomes better in this way and can have more delight for the way that he is better. Now since the temporal state as such necessarily limits the freedom of men for the sake of order and the common good, it is best that the temporal state does this less rather than more where this is possible. Yet at the same time, not all societies are the same, meaning that different societies can benefit in different ways from having different kinds of temporal states. It may be possible in one temporal state for men to have more freedom to act as they please, while in another temporal state it is necessary for the state itself to tell men more what to do for their own good. The degree of authority given to the temporal state in this way differs from one temporal state to another. Not all temporal states can be governed in the same way or even as the same kind of government.

That the temporal state can have more or less power over the people in the society necessarily relates to virtue. Virtue is when men act for the sake of the greatest possible good in every case, and they thus act for the delight that it can give them. Now when men live in society, to act with proper virtue also means they take into account the common good, since they can benefit from the common good no less than they can benefit from their particular good. And one of the ways that virtue can help men in a temporal society is to keep order among them. The temporal state itself emerges among the men in the society as one of the manifestations of order among the men themselves. As virtue conduces to order, the temporal state does not necessarily need to direct men as much if the men have more virtue. Hence a freer society is one in which the men can better order themselves without the help of the temporal state. But when the virtue of a society declines, the temporal state must take a greater degree of freedom from among the men in the society in order to keep the order for the whole society. So if a society declines because of a lack of virtue among men, the order will also disappear. And the lack of order means that the men lose their former freedoms because they could not keep order among themselves. So if men seek to live in a freer society, it is necessary for them to have proper virtue. No society in which the men lack virtue can last very long in itself, even taking into account the way that the temporal state has to direct the men more for the sake of order. The temporal state's greater need to direct men will keep the society alive for a short time longer, but it is not a permanent answer to the lack of virtue. And since the rulers of the temporal state come from among the people in the society and reflect their abilities, the rulers will not have much skill in keeping order when the men have lost their virtue. They might temporarily forestall the destruction of the society, but they cannot prevent it altogether.

Hence it is evident that virtue is necessary for men to function in a society, and it is also necessary to keep the temporal state within reasonable limits. That the temporal state or someone within the state itself exercises the final authority over all else does not have to mean that there is no freedom and that there are no other authorities to keep order among men. A better society has less direction coming from the temporal state and allows the men within the society to act more according to their own devices. But this depends upon the virtue of the men in the society, in the way that was said.

Since virtue itself ultimately concerns God, it is not possible or desirable for a society to ignore the obligations that men have to God as who they are. Virtue was said to be the desire for the greatest possible good in each case. And God alone is essentially good because being is the same thing as goodness and the Divine essence is existence Itself. Hence when men act with proper virtue, they choose what is more like God over what is less like God, since God alone is essentially good, and what is essentially so is more so than what is only according to participation. So men can use their desire for the greatest possible good in each case as a way to come closer to God in the end. And Christ Who is both God and man in the one hypostasis established the Church on earth as the means for men to come to God. It was already explained how all of the men who are saved in the end are saved because they were baptized into the Church on earth in one of the three forms of baptism. This is how there is no salvation outside of the Church. Now since the temporal state works for the common good of men, the common good comes about when men act with virtue, and virtue is properly directed to God as the ultimate end for the acts of men, it is clear that the temporal state properly directs men to live in accord with the sacred doctrine and practices of the

Church on earth. The spiritual is higher than the temporal because the spiritual can give men a greater delight than the temporal. As the lower exists for the sake of the higher, the temporal good is properly directed to the spiritual good for men. So if the temporal state is to properly fulfill its function to work for the common good of the society over which it rules, the temporal state has an obligation to form its laws in accord with Church doctrine. Just as the spiritual is over the temporal, the Church on earth must be set over the temporal state for the sake of the common good. This is the natural order for the temporal state.

At the same time that the temporal state owes this obligation to the Church on earth for the good of the society itself, this does not mean that a temporal state is illegitimate if it does not acknowledge the Church on earth as the religion of the state. Christ still told Pontius Pilate that Pilate had legitimate authority over Him even though Pilate was an agent of a pagan state. Hence it can be said that a temporal state that does not properly acknowledge the Church on earth is still a legitimate state all the same. But the temporal state in such cases fails to work for the common good of the men in the society to the fullest degree possible. So the temporal state does not fulfill its purpose to the degree that is possible to it, even though it does not for that same reason lack legitimacy.

For the most part, it is only possible for the temporal state to acknowledge the Church on earth as the state religion if most or all of the men in the society have been baptized into the Church on earth. It is not strictly necessary that all of the men in the society are among the baptized. This can still happen even if most of the men in the society have been baptized. The temporal state can still encourage the other men through the laws to enter into the Church on earth for the sake of their own good. Now since the temporal state can allow for some degree of pragmatic religious toleration for the unbelievers within the society, it is necessary to consider the obligations of the temporal state to the unbelievers. Men can truly come into the Church on earth by their own free will. Thus a forced conversion is no conversion at all, since it is not possible for the man to receive the Divine grace and virtue unless he is open in his free will to receive it. And the free will of a man in this case cannot be forced. Neither should the man be coerced so that he converts, because this would reduce the degree of his grace and virtue in the conversion itself. This would be for the temporal state to act contrary to the common good that the temporal state is meant to uphold. Thus the temporal state can give some pragmatic religious toleration to men not in the Church on earth. Yet for the good of the faithful who have been baptized into the Church on earth, the ability of unbelievers to either publicly practice or to proselytize among the men in the Church on earth can be limited or forbidden in the interest of the common good. The degree to which these other acts are allowed within the society is a matter of prudential judgment for the rulers, meaning that they can make their own decisions about how much pragmatic toleration is granted to the unbelievers.

The case for the men who have not been baptized into the Church on earth is altogether different from the cases of heretics or apostates. For the good of the society, the temporal state acknowledges the Church on earth as the state religion. But when some men become either heretics or apostates from the Church on earth, they challenge the authority of the Church on earth. Now since the temporal state depends upon the Church on earth, this is a threat to the temporal state as well. The temporal state properly punishes the men who challenge its authority because the temporal state exists to work for the common good of the whole society. Hence to undermine the authority of the temporal state is generally bad for the society, meaning that the temporal state can prosecute such people in the interest of the common good. So when Church authorities have found that a man has become either a heretic or an apostate, it is proper that he is also punished by the temporal authorities for the sake of his own good. And it is within the jurisdiction of the temporal state to decide what kind of punishment to inflict upon the heretic or apostate for the crimes of which he is guilty. He can and ought to be given the possibility to repent of his sins to come back into the Church on earth, in which case he could either be released from punishment or suffer a lesser degree of the punishment for what he did so that he can make up to the society for his crime. But in the event that the heretic or apostate does not repent of his sins and return to the Church on earth, more severe measures can be taken as punishment. This can mean execution. The soul is more important than the body, and the temporal society justly executes murderers and other criminals who commit comparably severe crimes. This is an act of justice by the temporal state that works for the common good. This means that the society itself offended by the crime is once more made whole because the criminal made up for his crime by paying with his life. Since the body is less important than the soul, it stands to reason that the men who kill the soul by heresy or apostasy deserve execution even more than murderers or men who commit other crimes against the body. This way the temporal state does justice to the heretic or apostate for what he did to the Church on earth and the way that he undermined the authority of the temporal state that works for the common good of the whole society.

This does not mean that all heretics or apostates from the Church on earth necessarily have to suffer execution for their crimes. But it does mean that the temporal state can have recourse to punishments in general and execution in particular in the event that this appears to be necessary for the particular case. It is a matter of prudential judgment to be taken by the temporal authorities in accord with the laws of the temporal state in the same way that they would punish other criminals who compromise the material good of the men in the society by their acts. Yet it remains the case that there is certainly no moral objection whatsoever to the execution of a man who has fallen into either heresy or apostasy from the Church on earth. That these punishments are used by the temporal state can help to keep the men in the society within the Church on earth and within proper virtue for the sake of their own good. This is the purpose for which the temporal state exists, and which cannot be properly fulfilled without the help of the Church on earth.

While it is best for the society that the temporal state rules to be religiously unified so that most or all of the members of the society are also in the Church on earth, it is not strictly the case that a temporal state needs to rule over a society of only one culture. It has long been the case throughout history that different temporal states included many different societies of diverse cultures. And since it is better for the temporal state to allow the people within the society to do more to rule over themselves, the different cultures under the temporal state can all have some degree of autonomy in order for them to be ruled more in accord with their own customs. It is not necessary that each culture have its own temporal state apart from the other temporal states that exist on earth. In some cases this can work better because the men within the society all share the same customs, meaning it will be easier for them to work together within the temporal state. But there are other cases when the temporal states that have been formed rule over many different cultures at the same time. Such arrangements can actually work well for all of the different cultures that are involved with each other while living within the bounds of the one temporal state.

At the same time that a temporal state can include more than one culture, it is also the case that the different cultures within the temporal state all have a right to protect their respective ways of life both from each other and from the other cultures of people who might come to live within their temporal state. While men have a natural right to leave one place for another for the sake of their own good, the movement of men from one place to another can be regulated by the temporal states. The temporal state itself has an obligation to preserve the cultures of the people who live under its authority. The different cultures themselves all have a natural right to preserve themselves from intrusion by outsiders within proper limits. Hence if there are new people that seek to live within the context of a culture different from their own, the people in the culture where they have settled can limit the number of new people so that their culture is not taken over by the new people who come to live among them. And the new people who come to live in a different society must respect the way of life of the people who live in their new home. They should treat the people of that culture with gratitude for allowing them to live among them. They should do what they can to minimize their impact on the rest of the society that has allowed them to settle among them. Different cultures have a natural right to preserve themselves from being taken over by other cultures, much in the same way that individual men can preserve their own personal good to some degree without having it taken away by other men. Since the temporal state exists to uphold the common good of the whole society, the temporal state has an obligation to recognize and preserve the cultures of the different societies that exist under its rule.

      The temporal state itself has a right to preserve its existence from being taken over by other temporal states around it. This was already mentioned concerning the way that heretics and apostates undermine the authority of the confessional temporal state. Now if another temporal state commits an act of aggression against it, the temporal state can respond by fighting a war to protect itself and its people. There are five conditions that must be met in order for a war to be just. First, the war must be a last resort after all peaceful options have failed. This way all that could be done has been done to prevent any suffering that arises from the war. Second, the war must be declared by a legitimate authority in order for the people to wage war. Third, there must be a reasonable chance of victory in the war so that the war does not cause unnecessary suffering. Fourth, the fighting must be restricted to the militaries rather than causing any undue harm to civilians. Fifth, a war should only be waged defensively rather than for the sake of conquest.

All of these conditions together are necessary for a just war. If even one of them is lacking, the conflict itself cannot be considered just. But that a war in general can be just derives from the natural right of men, both individually and socially, to work for the sake of their own good. No man can ever be morally bound to suffer humiliation, destruction, or capitulation contrary to his own good. This is entirely opposed to the way that virtue is for the sake of the greatest possible good of the man himself.

Thus war takes place when the ordinary peaceful means of interaction between temporal states have broken down. But most of the time it is possible for temporal states to peacefully interact with each other for their mutual benefit. In this case it is possible and desirable for the temporal states to work out laws among themselves for their common good, so that they can all work together to uphold the rules that they have decided upon among themselves. This is admittedly a different system than when an authority in the temporal state works for the good of its own people. In such cases there is a final authority set above all of the others for the sake of maintaining order and enforcing the laws. When different temporal states act in this way, there is no such authority because all of the different temporal states are on the same level with each other. Hence they have to interact by means of treaties and other agreements for the sake of upholding the common good among them. But since it is possible for there to be such systems among different temporal states, if one or more of the temporal states violates the laws that were established among them, then the other temporal states can take prudential measures to bring the disobedient temporal state into line with the laws. And war is possible for the sake of upholding such agreements among the different temporal states subject to the conditions of a just war that were already explained. But once the war or dispute has been settled, it is in the best interest of the temporal states to establish peaceful relations among them and not to try to punish the temporal states that have been brought back into line with the established laws.

One of the ways that temporal states can work to punish a state that defies certain laws is by conquest. First, if a temporal state is defying the natural law by which all men are bound, other temporal states can possibly intervene to protect the people of that temporal state from their own rulers. The rulers would have forfeited their legitimacy in this way by how they acted contrary to the higher law by which they were also bound, meaning that other temporal states can invade and take over for the sake of the people who live there. Second, conquest is acceptable if the rulers of a temporal state persecute the faithful in the Church on earth, since the Church on earth was said to be necessary for the temporal state to work for the good of its own people. Hence to persecute the faithful in the Church on earth is always contrary to the good of the temporal state. This means that the temporal state has attacked the Divine law itself as embodied within the sacred doctrine and practices of the Church on earth. This is another occasion when one temporal state can take over another. Third, conquest can be done if the people conquered lacked a temporal state of their own to work for their common good. This way the conquering temporal state can better work for the good of the people that it brings under its own rule. Fourth, it may be the case that the people of a particular society want to be incorporated into another society. Since the authority of the temporal state derives from God through the people who give their consent to the existence of the temporal state, the annexation of one temporal state by another is legitimate with the consent of the people who live in the society taken over. But if any of these four conditions is not the case, it is not moral for one state to conquer another, because this would take away the natural right of the society itself that was taken over to form its own temporal state for the sake of its own good. And more autonomy for societies is better because this conduces more to proper virtue, which is how men can become good and have more delight in their lives.

Since it is the task of the temporal state to work for the common good of the men over whom it rules, the temporal state can punish men in the interest of justice when the men have defied the just laws of the temporal state itself. The punishment makes the society itself whole again. It is the nature of the crimes established by the temporal state that they affect not just the individual men directly affected by the event, but rather all of the men who live under the rule of the temporal society. Hence it is proper that the temporal society, as the common expression of the will of the society itself, punishes the men who have transgressed its laws. And it is within the power of the temporal state to impose certain punishments that most closely accord with the degree of the good that was lost when the crime was committed. It was said that justice is based on equality, so that a thing gets the equal of what it deserves for what it is. So if a man commits a crime, he deprived the temporal state of some good when he disobeyed the law. This means that the temporal state can take some good from him in equal measure for the good of which the society itself was deprived. And this does not rule out the possibility that the temporal state can execute men for the crime of murder or other similarly serious crimes. The common good of the whole society is greater than the individual good because it is the good for a greater number of people. If the criminal has shown by his actions that his continuing to live is a liability as opposed to an asset to the whole society, it is proper for him to be executed once he has been duly convicted of breaking the law. This can also show other criminals that they can suffer the same end if they were to commit those crimes. In the event that the execution of a criminal is not a deterrent to crime, it is still the case that the execution made the society whole again. For the good that the criminal took by the crime he committed, he paid back to the society with his life. Hence he is no longer indebted to the society for the crime that he committed, even if this was only possible because he had to be executed for what he had done. This is all that is needed for the execution to be considered just.

There may be certain times when the temporal rulers of a society have shown by their acts that they no longer work for the common good of the whole society. When this happens, the people in the society have a natural right to depose their rulers and replace them with new ones, either while maintaining the same overall constitution or replacing it with a new one that they believe will work better to uphold their common good. For the temporal state to be overthrown can only be done in the most extreme cases, such as when the temporal rulers defy a higher law such as the natural law or the Divine law. If the misrule is only in prudential matters, it is not possible for the temporal rulers to be overthrown. The temporal rulers may appear incompetent in what they do, but since the rest of the people in the society do not have the same information that they do, what was done by prudential judgment may actually be good for the society itself. Ultimately in prudential matters, it is not possible for the men in the society to say if what is done is good or bad because they lack the same information that belongs to the rulers as such. So it is only in cases when a higher law is explicitly disregarded that the people of the temporal state can revolt against their rulers. In those cases the rulers have forfeited their legitimacy and thus lose the power that they had over the society. The society can even possibly execute the rulers if the offense of the rulers against the society was to such a degree that this is warranted. The rulers would be guilty of acts that were so immoral that the only way they could make up to the society is to accept execution.

Yet given the drastic nature of such a revolt, as well as the possibility of a breakdown of order in the society itself, this should only be a last resort for the society to defend itself against its own rulers.

These are the different matters that concern the human ability to make laws. Man is a social animal, meaning that he can use this social ability together with his rational intellect to form laws to bind the men within human societies. It has been shown the different ways that men can form temporal states to work for their own good, the ways that the temporal state can act in this manner, and the ways that men can respond to when the temporal state fails to uphold the good as the end thereof. It has also been shown how the temporal state depends upon the Church on earth as the state religion in order to work more effectively for the common good of the men in the society. But at the same time, the absence of the Church on earth as the state religion does not invalidate the legitimacy of the temporal state. All of these different matters have thus been considered here.

This treatise has shown that the entire created world is governed by different laws on different levels. All laws and all authority in general come from God as the first cause and as the one Who sustains all things in being by their nature as what they are. It has been shown that there are certain characteristics that belong to all law in general. And it has been shown how law can be divided as being either the eternal law, the natural law, the Divine law consisting of the Old Law and the New Law, and human law. The different topics that relate to each of them have been considered in due course, as well as the way that they all relate to God as both the beginning and the end for all things.

Milton Keynes UK
Ingram Content Group UK Ltd.
UKHW020657070823
426447UK00015B/689